e for *The Sacred Science*

"The Sacred Science *is a fresh narrative about healing that is at once ancient and pioneering. If you desire a deep dive into the psychological blind spots that may block your potential to heal—particularly when conventional medicine has failed you—read this book. Polizzi is in a class by himself as a scholar of ancestral medicine, a gifted storyteller brimming with integrity."*

— **Sara Gottfried, M.D.**, *New York Times* best-selling author of *Younger, The Hormone Cure,* and *The Hormone Reset Diet*

"Part adventure book, part self-help book, part memoir, part guide into the deepest parts of your soul . . . The Sacred Science *by acclaimed filmmaker Nick Polizzi will keep you on the edge of your seat as you explore the deep wisdom found in our world's ancient traditions. A Must Read."*

— **Nick Ortner**, *New York Times* best-selling author of *The Tapping Solution*

"Rarely are readers given the gift and opportunity to be introduced to the deep wisdom and healing that the universal practice of shamanism embraces. In The Sacred Science, *Nick Polizzi honestly shares how native rituals immerse us in both the light and the shadow, carrying us through to a place of illumination. This book demonstrates the raw and authentic power of shamanism without trying to soften what is required to truly engage in such an ancient tradition that can provide healing in ways many never imagined.*

Polizzi and the brave souls he brought with him ventured together into the jungles and experienced the magic of this earth-based practice. Read this book slowly, absorb and digest the inspirational wisdom. The Sacred Science *truly honors the sacredness of shamanic work."*

— **Sandra Ingerman, M.A.**, author of *Soul Retrieval* and *Medicine for the Earth*

"In The Sacred Science, *Nick Polizzi tells a riveting tale of exploration, hope, and wonder through his adventures into the Amazon. A regular guy from Connecticut follows his own health journey and finds the earth's greatest treasure—forgotten healing plants and the native cultures who know how to use them. It was hard to put this book down and the ending delivered a wallop that everyone needs to experience."*

— **Dr. Pedram Shojai**, *New York Times* best-selling author of *The Urban Monk*

THE
SACRED
SCIENCE

NICK POLIZZI

THE SACRED SCIENCE

AN ANCIENT HEALING PATH FOR THE MODERN WORLD

HAY HOUSE, INC.
Carlsbad, California · New York City
London · Sydney · New Delhi

Published in the United States by: Hay House, Inc.: www.hayhouse.com®
Published in Australia by: Hay House Australia Pty. Ltd.: www.hayhouse.com.au
Published in the United Kingdom by: Hay House UK, Ltd.: www.hayhouse.co.uk
Published in India by: Hay House Publishers India: www.hayhouse.co.in

Cover design: Michelle Polizzi
Interior design: Draft Lab/Alex Head
Indexer: Jay Kreider

Library of Congress has cataloged the earlier edition as follows:

Names: Polizzi, Nick, author.
Title: The sacred science : an ancient healing path for the modern world / by
    Nick Polizzi.
Description: 1st edition. | Carlsbad : Hay House, Inc., 2018.
Identifiers: LCCN 2017049357 | ISBN 9781401952914 (hardcover : alk. paper)
Subjects: LCSH: Shamanism.
Classification: LCC BF1611 .P645 2018 | DDC 201/.44--dc23 LC record available
at https://lccn.loc.gov/2017049357

Tradepaper ISBN: 978-1-4019-5293-8
E-book ISBN: 978-1-4019-5292-1
Audiobook ISBN: 978-1-4019-5387-4

10 9 8 7 6 5 4 3 2
1st edition, April 2018
2nd edition, March 2019

Printed in the United States of America

To my wife, Michelle, who taught me how to laugh from the heart, no matter what life brings. And to my two sons, River and Rowan, the greatest teachers I've ever known.

This one is for you.

CONTENTS

Note to Reader xi

Introduction 1

CHAPTER 1: Descent 7

CHAPTER 2: Initiation...21

CHAPTER 3: Crisis and Ceremony 31

CHAPTER 4: The Wall..55

CHAPTER 5: Arrival 71

CHAPTER 6: Medicinal Herbs and How the Shamans Find Them 81

CHAPTER 7: The Jungle Healing Diet 91

CHAPTER 8: Life and Death 111

CHAPTER 9: Relámpago 123

CHAPTER 10: Grandfather 137

CHAPTER 11: Breaking Down to Break Through.............. 151

CHAPTER 12: Wired for Tribe 165

CHAPTER 13: Ascent... 177

CHAPTER 14: Departure 201

Epilogue... 215

Bibliography.. 217

Index 219

Acknowledgments 229

About the Author 231

NOTE TO READER

Woven throughout this book are practices and other pieces of native wisdom that you can put to use in your life right now. These practices were shown to me by the healers you are about to meet, and it is with their permission that I've included them in this book.

Please, for your safety and the safety of those around you, be careful when experimenting with these techniques. They can be life-changing but can also do harm if used improperly.

INTRODUCTION

The afternoon heat in this place never disappoints. My left eye blinks away a nagging bead of sweat while trusty fore-finger and thumb locate and remove a mosquito on the skin just above my sticky T-shirt collar. The breed in these parts comes handily equipped with an anesthetic on its proboscis that numbs you as it drains your blood, so you don't feel the itch until the feast is over.

No free lunches in this place, señor.

I'm seated on the edge of a simple wooden chair tucked in the corner of a thatch-roofed jungle kitchen somewhere along the Amazonian border of Brazil and Peru—staring down the barrel of a very intimidating albeit colorful jug of liquid. The weathered brown hands of the native fellow holding it out in front of me speak to the decades he has spent navigating the bush, like the generations who have come before him.

His name is Arturo and he is the village *curandero*. Men and women of this ancient profession are thought to have an extrasen-sory relationship with the local plant spirits, which allows them to harness their power to cure the sick. I've heard it said that true curanderos, or shamans, are born with this skill and have little choice but to follow the calling.

Arturo, who comes from a long line of medicine men, promised to bring me some of his family's legendary elixir for strength and vitality. And, well, here it is.

The liquid inside the repurposed two-liter soda bottle on the table before me is mostly transparent, revealing a cluster of twigs, leaves, seeds, and insect thoraxes floating within.

"This is what men and women in my tribe drink every day before we go out to work. It's got 20 different ingredients and packs quite a kick. We also use it to heal head pain." Arturo holds the bottle up to the light, proudly identifying each of the floaters and sharing a bit about what they do to enhance the brew's potency.

The word *heal* is a tricky one. These four letters seem straightforward in the modern world, but around here, healing can involve just about anything—from a bandage and some aloe on a scraped knee to an all-night plant ceremony that brings you as close to your existential edge as you can get, short of death itself.

Heal stems from the old English word *hal*—which evolved into two other terms as well, *whole* and *holy*. Ten years ago, I would have thought these three words were totally unrelated, but staring into the eyes of the shaman before me, I now know better. They're as intertwined as the jet-black braid resting on his left shoulder.

"Are those insects in there?" I ask, knowing the answer.

"These? Fire ants! They have a painful bite, but their bodies contain powerful medicine. Really good for you."

I smile and nod with feigned excitement.

He twists off the fat plastic cap with an "Inca Kola" logo on it, and to our surprise, the bottle burps out an effervescent hiss, like a bottle of, well, Inca Kola.

"*Salud.*" Arturo pushes the bill of his well-worn trucker hat back from his brow and brings the full bottle to his lips, lifting the butt end high in the air. One, two, three, four, five strong pulls later, he lets out a long "Ahhhh . . ."

Followed by "Ooheee, this is a strong batch!"

Then it's my turn. "*Prueba, mi amigo,*" he urges. Judging by the look of casually disguised queasiness on the face of Arturo—who grew up drinking this stuff—I'm fairly confident it will not be a dull experience.

There's a special mental place I like to go to in moments like this. My line of work calls for a mildly insane streak to begin with, but repetition helps hone a peculiar skill that allows you to jump into these rabbit holes with less resistance from all those pesky survival instincts.

This is a place of no thinking. There is no benefit in fearing or speculating what will happen next, nor is there a shortcut around these obstacles—they are precisely where your path is meant to take you. The only thing to do is step forward and be ready for anything.

A Taoist priest once shared a piece of wisdom that I find myself reaching for as Arturo offers his potion, about a student of kung fu and his master. As the student's training advanced, his master would come at him with increasingly intense flurries of punches and kicks, fists thrusting through the air interspersed with painful blows from able feet.

The student's natural inclination was to try and calculate what the master would do next, but the dance unfolded too quickly for formulaic thought, each second loaded with 5 to 10 strikes that could come from any direction. If the master ever sensed that his pupil was using a patterned defense against his attacks, the punishment would be severe.

"Never anticipate," said the master. "Always be ready."

"*Salud.*" I nod at my smiling friend, hoping I'm hiding my own preemptive queasiness better than he's hiding his. Up goes the bottle, and down goes the long-lost elixir of youth.

■　■　■

The following true story is told through the eyes of an average white American male from New England who thought he knew something about himself and this world.

Until he dipped a toe into the world of shamanism and realized rather suddenly that he did not.

In this book you will meet a number of odd characters. Among them are two shamans, a *vegetalista* with an encyclopedic mind for medicinal jungle plants, a band of eight fearless patients willing to do anything to heal their illnesses, and my rough-and-tumble film crew.

You may be asking yourself, what business does an ordinary guy from Connecticut have trekking through the pristine tropics of South America? Very good question.

My name is Nick, and after healing naturally from a serious health challenge in my mid-20s, I decided to dedicate my life to an exploration of the ancient healing arts. This journey took me to the corners of the world, into the villages and homes of indigenous people who still use the sacred medicines and ceremonies of their ancestors.

Somewhere along the way, fate landed a camera in my hands, and it became apparent that guerrilla-style documentary filmmaking was a great way to preserve this fast-fading shamanic knowledge and bring these vital healing secrets to those in need of them.

But some things are too expansive to be adequately captured on film, and anyone who has spent time in the tribal lands of the Amazon jungle or neighboring Andes Mountains will tell you there is enough mystery here to fill lifetimes of exploration. So I'll be lending you the twenty-twenty lenses I was born with in my eye sockets for the ensuing chapters, as we dive into an unlikely healing expedition that was supposed to be an intrepid documentary but turned out to be a portal of infinite transformation.

My crew and I thought we were setting off to make a daring movie that would put the indigenous medicines of the rain forest to the ultimate test on *real patients*. It never occurred to us that we'd have to rewire our reality and confront the forgotten parts of ourselves in the process.

■ ■ ■

This book is all about shamanism, a word that is shrouded in mystery and often misinterpreted. So, before we get too far ahead of ourselves, let's get clear on what exactly the term means. The word *shaman* itself is Tungusic, originating in the remote Altai Mountains of Siberia. It translates literally to "one who knows."

In the traditions of Siberia, Mongolia, and parts of China, the word is used to describe an individual who bridges the physical world and the realm of spirits in order to bring balance to their tribe and heal the sick. They accomplish this by entering altered states of consciousness, whether induced by drum, psychoactive plant medicine, controlled exposure to enclosed heat, or other environmental aid.

Anthropological evidence of shaman figures can be found in cultures all around the world, dating back to our prehistory on this planet. One such example lies in a 5,000-year-old cave painting in Tassil, Algeria, that depicts a shaman with the head of a bee, surrounded by mushrooms. Older cave paintings found in France and Spain depict hybrid animal-humans that many historians believe are shamanic in nature as well.

The name used to describe this position of healer-priest in society varies with the native language of each particular region, but remarkably, the basic role and techniques used do not. A large number of the rites used by medicine men and women from different corners of the world are undeniably identical, aimed at pulling back the veil of this reality in order to purify the patient from within.

Hard-liners argue that because true shamanism originated in the forests of Siberia and Mongolia, only the native healers from these regions should be referred to as shamans. But native healers from the Americas, Africa, Australia, and Europe with similar practices utilizing altered states are often referred to as shamans as well because the term so precisely describes their craft.

Shamanism is often referred to as a lineage of direct transmission because shamanistic knowledge is passed down by word of mouth from generation to generation, without any written account. In teaching an apprentice, a shaman not only shows him or her the ceremonial practices and medicinal herbs, but also demonstrates how to *be* in this world.

Shamans are a living bridge between this dimension and the one we cannot see. Their fate is predetermined by their bloodline or through an unintended initiation, which usually manifests as a close encounter with death. I have grown to know and deeply respect a number of these men and women. But they do not share their knowledge lightly.

Centuries of oppression as well as the exploitation of native traditions have all but wiped out these lineages. The true wisdom keepers that remain have learned to keep their ancestral knowledge safe, sharing it only with a select few whom they trust.

One cardinal rule of the documentary filmmaker is to earn the trust of your subject while never forgetting what your job is: to document, not participate. But when it comes to highly sacred and often private shamanic ceremonies, not participating can be harder than it sounds.

Chapter 1

◇◇◇◇◇◇◇◇◇◇◇◇◇◇◇

DESCENT

*If we surrendered to earth's intelligence
we could rise up rooted, like trees.*

—RAINER MARIA RILKE

June 18, 2016
Larapata, Peru

I'm in a pickup truck on a one-lane dirt road hugging the side of a cliff about 16,000 feet above sea level, in the middle of the Andes Mountains. We're on our way to a remote region where the majestic highlands plummet suddenly into a flat sea of Amazon jungle green.

Roman, a 38-year-old shaman, is at the wheel, honking the horn as we whip around each blind turn to make sure any oncoming trucks know to stop. We're in a bit of a hurry, with only 90 minutes of daylight left and a two-hour hike at the end of this ride before we reach what Roman affectionately calls "the Land."

Nestled in one of the seemingly infinite valleys along this eastern slope is the new home of the Paititi Institute, where our documentary, *The Sacred Science*, was filmed. We're going to be doing a few ceremonies with the shaman's apprentices there, both ayahuasca and coca, and also filming some of the healers in the region.

Little do we know that getting to Paititi will be just as medicinal as the center itself.

We will be descending 4,000 feet on foot, through three different climate zones, into the Mapacho River Valley, then crossing two rope bridges before finally climbing partway up the other side of the valley and into the camp. This arduous new journey is a far cry from arriving at the institute's previous location, where a van could take visitors from a small airport all the way to the Paititi grounds.

As our Toyota Hilux rumbles down the narrow gravel road, the alpine vegetation around us begins to change to a lusher, more tropical variety. We're getting closer to the Amazon, and can feel the moisture and warmth blowing up the mountain and into the small truck's open windows.

Twenty minutes later, we reach an outpost farming village of about 200 people—the last semblance of civilization until we reach Paititi. Roman has a contact in town who stores the truck on his land and provides mules and pack horses to transport supplies down into the valley. While my colleague Mileen and I strap our backpacks on, Roman asks a few locals if they can pack the food and equipment we have in the bed of the pickup onto the animals and bring it down the following day.

It's never reassuring when the local Quechua, who know these lands like the back of their hands, look at each other and chuckle at the prospect of a pair of foreigners and their shaman guide trying to descend into the wilderness that lies beyond. In the fading light of a setting Peruvian sun, no less.

But these trips to Paititi are always a lesson in trust. Trust in Mother Nature and trust in the divine plan.

Onward.

As we begin our descent, Roman warns that going down will be much more challenging than coming back up, because of the unrelentingly steep incline. If you don't bend your legs with each step, using only your thigh and calf muscles to absorb impact, your knees will be shot in no time.

Down we go, carefully placing each foot on the path below, pushing ourselves to move more rapidly than we would ordinarily dare on terrain like this, as we race against the disappearing daylight. The old Incan route is barely wide enough for one person, carving its way along a perilous valley wall that drops sharply for miles until it ends abruptly at a thin blue stretch of river far below. The left side of the trail is adorned with all manner of plant life, but the right is nonexistent, the earth underfoot ending just inches away from certain death. Dropping into beautiful patches of wildflowers, golden blades of alpine high grass, and clusters of wild strawberries, we keep a wary eye on the ledge that lies just one misplaced footstep away.

About 20 minutes in, we come upon the ruins of an ancient Incan fortress strategically perched on a ridge with a commanding view of mountains and valleys in all directions. Mindful of the time, we admire it on the go, stopping for only a moment to take it in.

Thirty minutes later, we begin to hear the faint rumble of the Mapacho River far below. Roman yells back to us that we are halfway there. I can't tell by his cheery tone of voice whether or not he's toying with us. I yell back that I don't believe him, but he stops momentarily and gives me the medicine man look that I've come to know means he's not playing around.

Daylight is just about gone, and now we're in a little bit of a pickle. We're tired—and being tired while traversing a challenging mountain trail is a recipe for potential disaster. But if we slow down, we'll be trying to navigate the walls of this valley in complete darkness.

About 50 feet ahead, Roman yells back, "Okay, we're about to enter the most difficult stretch. Pay very close attention to what you are doing. Pure presence. Don't get distracted."

I echo Roman's words back to Mileen, who is stepping quickly through the dusk about 50 feet behind me. He responds with a partly intelligible "Got it," presumably not wanting to waste any more air than is necessary.

Once we've traversed the ridge, we see immediately what Roman was talking about. The trail goes from packed earth to a steeper grade under loose rocks and an even steeper cliff to the immediate left side.

It gets to a point where there is no room for even the slightest thought or conversation of any sort—one of those situations when you know your life may hang in the balance with each second that passes.

We breathe harder as we go. It becomes too steep to walk so we accelerate into a crouched trot, our headlamps turned on and pointed at the ground directly underneath us.

I hear a subtle voice inside begin to chatter. *What in the hell have you gotten yourself into? You've gone too far this time.* Responding to the voice, I tense up momentarily, glance over the ledge down into the ravine, and trip over a rock underfoot. Lurching forward, I grab on to a small shrub to keep myself upright and on the path. Close one.

I involuntarily start repeating a mantra to myself: *One step at a time. Eyes on the path, not on the edge. My breath is my friend. Trust in nature.*

I say these words over and over to keep any other thoughts out of my mind and the fear at bay. As the terrain becomes more treacherous, the trot turns into more of a dance, each step following the rhythm of the mantra and conforming to the shape of each rock and curve ahead. No thinking, just doing, reacting, surviving.

The spirit of the valley courses through my body as fear gives way to joy.

A spirit gliding through the night begins to ask some rather innocent questions of the body it inhabits. *Whose nose is this that is smelling the warm high-jungle breeze? Whose brow is this, dripping with salty sweat?*

I've lost the understanding of who Nick Polizzi is and have gained the understanding of who *I* am. There's no ego left. I've become the valley around me. It might sound counterintuitive, but my built-in self-preservation instincts are not needed to stay alive on the mountain.

Up ahead, I see Roman's headlamp suddenly stop advancing and turn back at me. I approach the bright beacon in the dark. "Okay," he says in a winded voice. "The worst is behind us. We're almost there."

Twenty-five minutes later, we're crossing an old rope bridge that creaks as we walk over the turbid waters of the Mapacho River. The remaining quarter-mile hike partway up the other side of the ravine feels effortless compared with the descent. Before we know it, we're entering the Paititi camp, greeting the staff and students who wait for us.

■　■　■

That night, as we eat dinner with Roman and three of his apprentices, I share the experience of becoming "no one" on the mountain. Roman smiles a big, toothy grin. "It's amazing how fast our illusions fall away when our life is on the line, isn't it?"

We're sitting cross-legged on thick alpaca blankets in an adobe structure known as "the Temple." It's the largest building on this 2,500-acre plot, serving as both meeting space and dining hall for all the patients, students, permaculturists, and healers who work here. As the shaman speaks, I notice that two of his apprentices are sharing a separate reaction to my story. Elton, a former Michelin star–rated chef from the small island nation of Malta, is the first to speak, in a melodic accent.

"Nick, it's a beautiful coincidence that you lost track of who you were on your way down the valley. We choose one question to meditate on each night. Before you arrived, Anthony, Stella, and I chose tonight's question. Guess what it is?"

They all look at me, waiting for me to guess, before Anthony breaks the suspense and answers the question for me. "It's 'Who am I?'"

In another life, I would probably have looked skeptically at this type of coincidence, but the past five years have been a series of perfectly placed episodes of synchronicity. *The Sacred Science*, my documentary about Amazonian shamanism that brought Roman and me into each other's reality, was a spiderweb of undeniable coincidence that seemed impossible at first but has since become as normal as a starry night.

This is not to say that I take synchronicity for granted. It has become an indispensable navigational tool on this ancient road into the unknown, a shining beacon in the dark that always seems to show up when I'm exactly where I'm supposed to be. Like cairns on a mountain trail, these unexpected alignments of circumstance confirm that your compass and contour map are pointing you in the right direction.

I smile and half bow to the three apprentices, before turning to Mileen. "Looks like we came to the right place."

"Isn't it beautiful that we haven't even sat in tomorrow's ayahuasca ceremony yet and there are already major shifts happening for you?" Roman asks. "What a gift!" His eyes are a mixture of compassion and amusement—like he's watching his younger brother learn his way around a pack of firecrackers the hard way.

Roman and I have known each other for 10 years, during which time he's become one of my dearest friends, but moments like these are a humbling reminder that ours is also a shaman/student relationship.

"We don't grow by staying comfortable," Roman says. "When we're at our edge, whether in ceremony or on an Incan trail in the darkness, we learn who is really at the wheel."

But who *is* really at the wheel?

My position coming into this trip was that the ego—that facet of personality in charge of self-preservation—was a hindrance in spiritual matters but gravely important when it came to life-or-death situations and strategic choices. I'm not alone in that belief. Ever since Sigmund Freud put a name to it (and probably long before), scientists and naturopaths have generally agreed that the ego's core functions of judgment, control, planning, and defense are essential in keeping ourselves alive. But Roman takes issue with this model and has chosen it as a focal point for my "education" on this visit.

"You're going to have to learn that letting go and embracing the unknown isn't just something we do in ceremonies," he continues. "Every moment of your life is sacred and loaded with subtle information that can only be witnessed by one who has clear sight. This can only be gained by letting go of who we are and the fear-based anticipation of what might happen next."

Seeing what must be a look of confusion on my face, he dumbs it down for me. "You still think you need to drive the car, but the wise man knows that he *is* the car and the car *is* the road. You don't need to drive, Nick. You just need to trust."

His point finally starts to sink in, leaving me inspired but agitated—a feeling that I've experienced many times over the past decade on the medicine path. The good news is that this nagging "soul itch," usually brought on by a glimpse at something bigger than I have the capacity to integrate, tends to be a precursor to a personal breakthrough just around the corner.

The idea of letting your heart guide you always sounded like New Age quackery to me when I was younger, but with the help of some very humbling purification rites, I've learned the hard way that, contrary to popular belief, my brain is not the control center. My journey has become a lesson in sitting still, listening with my heart for subtle bits of guidance that my brain cannot and will never be able to process.

The descent into the Mapacho Valley had been a living lesson, an awakening demonstration of how humans releasing the ego and operating from somewhere beyond can indeed take better care of themselves, even in a harrowing test of physical resilience and agility. In the shaman's company, these conceptual teachings about higher humanity have an eerie way of manifesting themselves soon after the words are spoken, in real-life scenarios— which usually involve a healthy dose of fear.

Roman pats Elton on the shoulder and looks at the rest of us. "Let's head over to the chapel and chew some coca. It will be good to make an offering to Grandma and get used to the space before tomorrow's ceremony."

LETTING GO

The clearest way into the Universe is through a forest wilderness.

—JOHN MUIR

Ever have that feeling when you're walking in the forest and a sensation of home tingles up your spine? The natural world begins breathing you in and out, gently washing away all of your perceived problems, leaving you in a state of direct experience with the beauty that is.

Wandering through meadows or over meandering tree roots or along crumbling walls of rock, you begin to see correlations between this ecosystem and the inner workings of your own mind. The more present you become with the soil under your feet and the character of the air moving into and out of your lungs, the more obvious your stresses and life challenges become.

Everything in nature is in full communication. There is no one overseer. No hero and no villain. Everything that transpires here is part of an ever-evolving cycle.

Luckily, you don't need to take a trip to the Amazon to experience the essence of earth medicine. In fact, it can be far more empowering to do it in your own neck of the woods.

A NATURE IMMERSION EXERCISE:

A. Schedule 90 minutes this week to gift yourself. You will be embarking on a short voyage.

B. Before leaving your house, remove all items from your pockets or backpack that could be a distraction—including cell phone, computer, magazines, newspapers, iPod, notebook, etc.

C. Travel to a local forest or park.

D. Upon arrival, walk until you find a space away from any man-made stimuli, including other people. Sit down. There is no need to close your eyes; just be still.

E. If possible, remove your shoes and socks, letting your feet touch the earth.

F. Begin to watch the ticker tape of thought and notice how it fluctuates over the course of 90 minutes.

Some things you may want to pay attention to:

• How long does it take for your mind to become extremely quiet?

• What triggers your mind to become hyperactive?

• What thoughts, positive and negative, begin to come up?

• What can you sense about your immediate environment?

• If you are working through a particular health challenge, what thoughts are coming up around this?

If you listen with an open heart, the forest will begin to reveal its secrets to you—and along the way it might help you reveal some of your own secrets as well.

■ ■ ■

The six of us are sitting on the floor of a small Spanish chapel that must be at least 300 years old, making small talk by candlelight. The mountains of South America hold many small Christian holy structures like this one, no more than 10 feet across by 10 feet wide, with an ornate altar occupying the entire wall opposite the entryway.

When the conquistadors first invaded these lands, they noticed that the local Incan people had built shrines and temples on certain points in the highlands that they felt were places of power. People would gather at these sacred structures to pray and give offerings to the *apus,* the spirits or gods of each mountain, asking for protection and insight.

As a strategy to help force Catholicism on this mysterious civilization, the Spaniards simply replaced these ancient places of worship with chapels like the one we're sitting in. The conquistadors knew the natives would still come to the sacred place, regardless of what type of building was there, and would slowly begin to embrace the prayers, beliefs, and one god of the Catholic Church.

The chapels that remain today are things of beautiful simplicity, but the history and initial intention behind their creation are anything but.

BOOM.

The corrugated metal roof above us shudders as the wind picks up outside. It's hard to believe it will stay attached to the rafters. The original roof on this thing was probably more aesthetically pleasing and quiet.

The conversation stills as Roman nods to his apprentices and they begin to unfold their small and intricately woven mesa blankets onto the floor before us. Next, they each produce a bag of green leaves from their medicine sacks, untie them, and grab handfuls to place in the center of each mesa square. Next, they take out identical jars of fine greenish powder, which they place very reverently next to each pile.

"Seeing as we will be doing an ayahuasca ceremony here in this chapel tomorrow evening, I felt that it would be good for the six of us to have a coca ceremony to prepare the space tonight. This is a unique group of people who I feel are in high resonance with this path, and this is an opportunity for us each to connect and get better acquainted with this ancient structure."

We've been chewing coca leaves since we arrived in the Andean city of Cusco last week. Coca, the same plant that is synthesized into cocaine, is one of the most sacred plants in South

America, if not *the* most. It has been used for thousands of years as a medicine, food, and ceremonial sacrament and is what many *maestros* refer to as a power plant.

One thing is for sure, it's saved our asses these past few days.

The reason why almost every one of the Quechua woodsmen in the high Andes chews coca is because, among its many other virtues, the leaf prevents altitude sickness and gives a sustainable boost of energy. I've experienced the energizing effects of coca in the past, but it wasn't until I was 13,000 feet up in the mountains that I realized its altitude defying power.

Earlier today, as we were driving over a particularly high mountain pass, the car had gone quiet as Mileen and I were overcome with nausea. I began turning green. Roman shot me a quick glance from the driver's seat, then shook the bag of coca leaves next to him. "Keep chewing coca. Don't stop for a second up here. It's too high for us to keep moving at this pace without it."

Mileen and I did as we were told, stuffing a bunch into our cheeks along with a small spoonful of "activator"—a local mixture of ground leaves and baking soda. Within minutes the nausea and dizziness were completely gone.

Nothing like personal experience to substantiate the claims made around a traditional medicine.

"*Hallpay kusinchis,*" Elton says, speaking the traditional Quechua blessing as he leans across the intimately close chapel floor to Roman, offering three attractive leaves, pinched between index finger and thumb. His words translate in English to "Let us chew coca together."

"*Urpiay sunkayai,*" Roman replies, uttering the traditional response, which means "Fluttering doves from my heart." He gazes into Elton's eyes as he receives the offering.

The ceremony has begun.

In a traditional coca ceremony, each participant chooses three unblemished coca leaves from the pile before him or her and forms them into a small bundle, or *kintu*, making sure that each one is facing stem-down and green side toward the person who will receive it. The triad is then waved in front of the recipient's mouth while a prayer is blown into it by the giver. Once the bundle has been charged with a blessing, it is handed over.

As the six of us make kintus for one another, atop what might be an ancient Incan power portal, a feeling of peace descends on the room. I haven't met these apprentices before, but there is no impulse to ask them about their lives or tell them about mine. The fact that Roman has brought us all here to meet is evidence enough of who we are and what we believe in.

While we chew, he begins to tell the apprentices about Mileen and me. Roman spends a few minutes recounting how he and I made a documentary film about shamanism here in the Amazon a few years ago, a roller-coaster ride that somehow became a hit film.

Elton and Stella nod approvingly, mentioning that they've seen it. "Thank you for creating that beautiful film," Elton says. "I watched it when it was first released!" His eyes shimmer in the candlelight as he speaks.

I smile and nod, my eyes lowering for a moment, a habit I have become painfully aware of over the past couple of years. Creating the film took me the better part of two years and all the money I had (plus some hefty loans), and it has been viewed by more than two million people, spawning a thriving online community of seekers and natural medicine enthusiasts. Yet I still feel uneasy speaking about it with shamans, apprentices, and other native healers who are doing the real work on a daily basis.

"What is your purpose on this trip, Nick?" Anthony, who has been silent until now, looks straight into my eyes as he speaks.

Roman answers for me. "Nick is here to refine his process, see the essence of his and our work, and resolve some of the internal blocks that are still hindering him on his path."

I smile widely at the group with a big cheekful of coca. His words are the truth, and it feels wonderful to have my vulnerabilities spoken out loud in a safe environment. Surprisingly, I don't feel any pangs of shame or defensiveness.

With eyes trained on the candle in front of me, I add cautiously, "I'm hoping to ask Grandma for some guidance on a few issues in our ayahuasca ceremony tomorrow night. It's been a long time, and I've got a bunch of questions for her."

"I have a feeling you won't have any time to ask questions in tomorrow's ceremony," says Roman, carefully assembling his next kintu. "Grandma hasn't seen you in a while, and there will be some deep purging to do."

The shaman and his apprentices all laugh heartily at this, grinning at each other and back at me. "Grandma" is the affectionate (yet always reverent) name by which the shamanic community refers to ayahuasca, one of the most sacred—and certainly the most hallucinogenic—of the medicinal plants of the Amazon. And one rarely enjoys a visit with Grandma without first relinquishing the contents of their stomach. I do my best to laugh along with the others, but a familiar sense of dread is already beginning to set in.

It'll be 24 hours until we drink the vine of souls, but her medicine is already beginning to reach out to me. *Who in God's name would want to subject himself to the very real agony that Grandma Ayahuasca can bestow upon those who partake of her?*

As I sit there, my mind begins to engage in one of its favorite pre-ceremony pastimes, asking itself again how in the hell I got here.

Chapter 2

◇◇◇◇◇◇◇◇◇◇◇◇◇◇◇

INITIATION

*Your pain is the breaking of the shell
that encloses your understanding.*

—Khalil Gibran

never intended for any of this to happen.

I grew up Catholic in a small town in Connecticut, where the word *spirituality* meant going to church on Sundays, saying some quick prayers at night, and rushing through grace before supper on special occasions. Other than that, it wasn't spoken of much.

There is a coldness of climate and demeanor in New England that only locals truly understand. People mind their own business, and in doing so they expect you to mind yours. This makes for quiet cul-de-sacs, charming but stuffy school settings, and plenty of well-kept secrets.

It also creates awkwardness in places of worship.

I could never tell if anyone was happy to be in our church. Aside from the priests, deacons, and altar boys, nobody really spoke or engaged in conversation. This was just fine by me because it allowed my brain to zone out and think about other things while my body performed the memorized routine. I'd see other kids I recognized from school in adjoining pews as we went up to receive

Communion, but it was only minimally acknowledged with a quick glance, as if to say, "Oh, your family drags you here too."

Stand up, listen, recite the appropriate response, sit down and turn to a page from the prayer booklet, stand up and repeat a few more words, then sit, then stand and shake hands with your neighbor, then kneel this time instead of sitting, then get on line to eat a dry wafer, recite a few more lines, and then go home. Maybe football will be on.

My sister, Liz, and I always employed our own passive resistance strategies on Sundays. We'd take our sweet time getting ready, watching the clock in hopes that my mom and dad would become distracted and leave themselves too little time to make it to church. It was a fifty-fifty shot. Sometimes we got off the hook and quietly rejoiced. Other mornings, we piled into the car and got there early like good Christians.

Despite my dislike for the sermons at Saint Joe's, I prayed diligently on my own every night throughout my childhood. This felt far more important. Some people talk about having a conversation with God through their prayers, but mine were one-way transmissions.

I'd lie there in the dark and plead with him to watch out for my family and me and to forgive whatever I'd done wrong that day, and then I'd wrap it up with a Hail Mary and an Our Father. I wasn't rejoicing in the existence of a divine and almighty creator; I was taking out a nightly insurance policy against the possibility that someday I'd die and have to answer to Saint Peter for my transgressions, which were many.

I felt this same motive from the other churchgoers while we sat there in our ergonomically challenged church pews. It seemed they were all there because they were fearful of what might befall them if they weren't. Generations and generations of fire and brimstone had culminated in this awkward collective of middle-class Americans who felt obligated to congregate and repeat words out of a poorly stapled pamphlet.

My young mind had two main hang-ups with the religion I was born into. For starters, I couldn't get over the notion that a human being could behave as badly as he or she wanted to during the week and then get off scot-free by coming to church and confessing to a priest. I was convinced that this spiritual get-out-of-jail-free card had to be a man-made creation, not something from the heavens.

I didn't have to go farther than the church parking lot to observe that the people I saw on a weekly basis at church were living in total contradiction to the ideals their holy book espoused, and then showing up on Sunday to clean the slate. "It's easier for a camel to go through the eye of a needle than for a rich man to enter into the Kingdom of God," read the honorary lector who had arrived in a brand-new Beemer. Everyone agreed to "do unto others as you would have them do unto you" just moments after jockeying for the best parking spot and quietly cursing the jerk who cut them off at the intersection.

Second, and more important, I wasn't wired with the ability to accept how non-experiential it all was. Faith is the central pillar of the Roman Catholic Church, and I couldn't bring myself to trust that every word in the long book of God applied to me. I needed concrete proof that I was a soul being, temporarily occupying this capsule of flesh, bone, and blood called Nick.

There was no community, no kumbaya circle of acceptance or unconditional love and compassion. The old Bible movies that my grandparents lived by depicted beautiful collectives of early Christians, unified by their shared beliefs and mission to walk the earth emanating God's love. What transpired at Saint Joseph's Church on your average Connecticut Sunday looked nothing like that.

When I was 14, I noticed an odd-looking altar in Liz's bedroom that was adorned with candles, a few unrecognizable statues, a handwoven rug, and an oversize book with the word *Wicca* written across the front. It was definitely intriguing—but only because it validated my suspicions at the time that my sister was a weirdo.

I flipped through the book, taking in the drawings of naked women, pentagrams, and hoofed animals it contained. The magic spells, rituals, and vision-inducing plants of the earth goddess seemed very experiential and exotic, but it was like switching to the opposite team. Weren't these supposed to be the bad guys?

It felt like a bad '80s movie, and it basically was.

Spirituality left me altogether as I became a young man occupied with the usual distractions of an early twentysomething. College friends, drinking and drugs, studying enough to get decent grades, falling in love with girls, more drinking, and ultimately entry into the grind of the workforce.

Then, one day in late 2002, something happened that interrupted my ascent into middle-class obscurity.

I was sitting in front of a computer screen when suddenly everything in my vision went bright and blurry. Imagine the kind of blindness that happens after you accidentally stare into the sun for a moment. It was like that but gradually encompassed everything in my vision. I naturally panicked and began stumbling around trying to get to the bathroom and splash cold water on my face. And then, just as suddenly as it started, the blindness stopped and I could see perfectly again.

I had no idea what had just happened, but I did the first thing I usually do when medical things happen that I can't explain. I began to phone my mom. I was about halfway through dialing her number when my brain screamed in an explosion of excruciating pain. I involuntarily curled up into the fetal position on the floor, shuddering with every new wave of intensity.

I was in complete darkness in a soundless room for eight hours before the pain finally began to subside.

That week I took my first-ever trip to a neurologist and was told that I had experienced an ocular migraine headache. If you don't know what an ocular migraine is, I'll just say this: We're not talking about normal pain. This is a debilitating condition that can ruin your life, as it did mine for the first two years that I had them.

Imagine the feeling of pushing on a broken bone or muscle tear, but in the center of your brain, continuously, for six to eight hours.

The migraines would come on without warning, and the pain often reached such intensity that I'd lose the ability to form words or communicate. My girlfriend at the time witnessed many bouts of unnerving behavior during these spells.

One day she came home to our apartment to find me huddled under a blanket in the bedroom, unable to respond to anything she said. I tried to piece a sentence together, but all that came out was a garbled mess that didn't make any sense. It wasn't that I was mumbling; the actual words I was saying were random and wrong. I tried to tell her that I needed a glass of water, but all that came out was "Baseball. Dog. Hand it over."

My doctor, one of the most highly regarded neurologists in Connecticut, prescribed a number of different drugs to combat the headaches. Each would provide some temporary relief but ultimately lost its effect after about two migraine episodes. I went back to the doctor one day, and he told me that the only remaining option was to start taking a preventive medication that was only 50 percent effective and would certainly change my moods and alter my perception of reality.

That's where I got off the modern medicine bus.

It's interesting when life reveals a personal boundary that you never knew you had. I was anything but a naturopath at the time, but the idea of taking a medication that would change the way I perceived the world was completely out of the question, even if it meant bearing the brunt of this migraine pain without aid.

Oddly enough, these headaches would turn out to be the biggest blessing I've ever received. Through a series of unforeseeable events, they delivered me onto the shamanic healing path I now walk.

■ ■ ■

About a week after I gave up on modern medicine, I was in the middle of yet another serious migraine when the phone began to ring. I wouldn't usually pick up the phone during an episode, but I saw that it was my best friend, also named Nick. He knew what

I was going through and always had a bit of encouragement or sympathy that made me feel slightly better.

I mumbled hello and told him I was in the thick of a bad episode and had to go because it hurt even worse to talk. "I know it hurts, but please try something with me. I think I've got something that will help you." Nick told me he had just learned a natural pain-relief technique called EFT that was supposedly really effective for migraine pain—and that he could teach me how to do it right over the phone.

I agreed to stay on for another five minutes and give it a shot. A moment later he was instructing me on how to tap on different points on my face and upper torso while saying a series of affirmations out loud. It took every bit of strength I had to sit upright and follow his quirky DIY Chinese acupressure lesson, but about three minutes into it, he asked me a question that shook me to my core and awakened something that I'd never felt before. "If your pain were a person, who would it be?"

An image of a close family member flashed across my awareness along with a particular setting inside a car that I knew very well. I had had a painful argument with this individual over something this person had done that really disturbed me a few years earlier. As I watched this scene swirling through the static of migraine turmoil, I had an unexpected emotional release. Tears filled my eyes, and as they did, the madhouse inside my head quieted. The pain began to drain.

Within 10 minutes, 90 percent of my pain was gone. Nick was as flabbergasted as I was. "Wait, really?" he asked. "Dude, I told you this stuff worked!" I was astonished and exhausted. We spoke for a few minutes; then I got off the phone and fell into a deep sleep.

Apparently the intense emotions around this painful event had continued to burden me long after the actual encounter had passed. From that day on, the migraines became far less frequent, and when they did occasionally occur, the pain and other symptoms were milder than a normal headache.

The act of turning toward a blind spot in the shadows of my psyche and acknowledging its existence was a maiden voyage for me. Until then, I'd had no idea that it was possible to access the causes of personal suffering and work to alleviate them. With this one glimpse, I was quickly hooked. I had to keep on digging.

This pivotal migraine experience unlocked a new intuitiveness in me. Almost as if I had gained access to an extra sense, I now began seeing more subtle aspects of my reality that were out of balance. I began to examine all of my seemingly innocent habits, behaviors, and patterns for anything that elicited a "bad idea" response in my gut.

Within a few months of probing, I discovered that drinking coffee and eating sharp cheeses were the cause of the remaining 10 percent of my migraine headaches. So I stopped. And so did they.

This combination of ancient Chinese acupressure and some small alterations in my diet turned out to be more effective than any drug that I had tried. It had also unblocked a part of me that had been wounded for such a long time.

Oddly enough, this disruptive migraine saga is also how I got into filmmaking. Without the headaches, I would be somewhere else right now, doing something that isn't nearly as satisfying as writing this book.

■ ■ ■

Until the triumph over my chronic headaches at age 26, I'd never had a real calling in life. Early on, my folks pointed out that I was good at drawing, a craft that I honed on the pages of textbooks and the margins of test papers, ultimately landing me in design school. But this was just surface-level stuff. There was no real purpose or identification with something greater.

Natural medicine and the exploration of human consciousness wasn't a vocation; it was a path. My heart was tugging me toward something much larger than myself, showing me flashes of a life spent helping others see the tremendous power of ancestral healing methods.

You can go through your entire life without ever noticing that Buddhist temple down the street or the Ayurvedic herb shop a few towns over. They are part of somebody else's culture until the day you become a refugee of the belief systems you've been relying on—until the day you are desperately seeking answers in the face of a disease or crisis that isn't adequately addressed in the owner's manual you inherited from your family, your community, or your culture of origin.

The natural food shop down the street from my Park Slope apartment in Brooklyn became a mecca. The jars of herbs, shelves of books on Eastern philosophy, and overall demeanor of the individuals who ran it were therapeutic in themselves. After having put all my chips on modern medicine and lost, the world of folk medicine reached out and began to show me the old way of caring for oneself and for others who are sick.

The universe is funny. Once you're dialed in to a calling, the cosmic gears begin turning behind the scenes, ultimately aligning you with an improbable opportunity to express your gifts and serve your purpose.

Two friends, Kevin Gianni and Nick Ortner (the same Nick who helped me cure my migraines), called me up one day and said they were in the middle of making a documentary about the tapping technique that had healed me—EFT, or Emotional Freedom Technique. But they had hit a roadblock and needed some advice.

"Um . . . you need advice from me? What do I know about filmmaking?" I was sure they were kidding.

"You went to design school. Didn't you take any photography courses there?" I could tell by his tone that Ortner was actually being serious.

I laughed out loud. "You guys must be in a lot of trouble if the future of your film relies on my one semester of college photography."

"Listen, we've got a bunch of camera gear but we're not sure how to use it. Can you come out here and take a look?"

A day later, we were standing in a basement staring at a bunch of video and audio gear that was still in the box. I put my game face on and began pulling things out and assembling them. "Yeah, I can figure this out."

A month later, I had taken over the production side of the film, traveling around the country to interview a number of thrilling thought leaders in the world of health and wellness. We stood behind those cameras extracting empowering bits of wisdom from our subjects about the potential of the human organism to heal itself and were almost always left grinning with excitement after our subjects had left the room.

But as we started assembling the footage in the editing room, I realized there was something obvious missing—real patients using EFT and getting better.

Natural medicine is people's medicine. In 90 percent of the world, traditional approaches are still turned to first, before modern treatments are ever considered. Our work had to involve real people, putting this approach to the test in real time and speaking candidly about their experiences.

We decided to host a four-day healing retreat in a rural town in Connecticut, inviting 10 patients with varying ailments, from psychological conditions like PTSD and depression to chronic pain and breast cancer, to come and work with the best EFT practitioners in the world. Each day, our team filmed their healing journeys in the most unobtrusive manner possible, capturing not only the profound physical breakthroughs but the underlying mental and emotional transformations as well.

We were left with compelling documentary proof that it worked, as well as a living testament to the bravery of patients who are willing to confront the psychological blind spots creating disharmony in their lives.

It was my first film, and it shows, but we had pointed our cameras at something that was hard to look away from: real human beings putting it all on the line to get their lives back.

And like that, I became a documentary filmmaker in the world of health, wellness, and spirituality.

My modus operandi in the projects I take on is to focus on stories of real patients let down by modern medicine as they try a specific alternative therapy or natural medicine. This desire to prove the effectiveness of folk healing methods probably comes from the same place as my childhood intolerance for the religious indoctrination at Saint Joseph's—an absence of blind faith and a stubborn need for concrete, experiential evidence.

It could also be a simple longing, as a viewer of films, to see real people being honest about who they are and ultimately overcoming all odds.

Whatever the motive, this documentary approach is far less predictable than creating an archival "talking head" film. These are real patients who are putting their trust in you to help them, and we never take that lightly. This is a combination of consciously filmed reality and quasi-scientific experimentation with natural medicine, but it's always done in a highly controlled environment.

What I was about to propose for our next film was almost impossible to control, and about 100 times as risky.

The vision was to bring eight sick individuals into the middle of the Amazon rain forest, more than a thousand miles from what would pass as a modern hospital, to work with the undiscovered plant medicines of the indigenous shamans there.

My friends thought I was absolutely nuts, and in retrospect, I probably was.

Chapter 3

ⲟⲟⲟⲟⲟⲟⲟⲟⲟⲟⲟⲟⲟⲟⲟⲟⲟⲟ

CRISIS AND CEREMONY

Synchronicity is an ever-present reality
for those who have eyes to see.

—CARL JUNG

November 17, 2009
Brooklyn, New York

I'm in a crammed, makeshift office attached to my third-floor Brooklyn apartment, taking notes on an academic text by ethnobotanist Richard Evans Schultes. Window is open, fan is on, and the murmur of Flatbush Avenue traffic fills the room, occasionally punctuated by a siren or horn.

For months I've been poring over classical and contemporary texts about medicine men, bonesetters, wise women, and shamans from different cultures in North and South America and around the world. I'm learning about the medicines they use, the ceremonies they perform, the rites of initiation they must go through, delving night after night into just about every text about native medicine and spiritual rites that I can get my hands on. I've been mapping out any tribes across the globe that have a lineage of ancestral knowledge that is still partially or fully intact.

I'm overcome with an itch that is probably familiar to most journalists and documentarians. Shamanism is where our next film is, but I can't seem to find my way into it.

If the goal were simply to document shamans and their sacred practices, I would assemble a film team and venture off into the outback of any of the six non-icy continents, letting the story unfold as we investigated. But this is not that type of project.

The small team that I've assembled so far (my girlfriend, Michelle, an art director at HBO; my cousin Dan, a producer at CNN; and little old me) is in unanimous agreement about what would make for the most compelling—albeit slightly insane—documentary. Our plan is to bring eight patients with serious illnesses to some remote region of the planet where a group of indigenous healers will attempt to make them well using traditional methods. It's a total reach and fraught with potential disaster, but there has never been a documented trial of the healing practices used in indigenous cultures. To the contrary, these tribes are considered to be primitive and uneducated, despite the fact that many of our modern medicines are derived from plants that *they* discovered and generously shared with Ivy League botanists.

In our eyes, there is only one way to do this film right: with real people, real illnesses, real cures.

We've decided that our target region of the world will be the Amazon rain forest. Not only does this gigantic stretch of wilderness hold countless shamanic traditions that are still alive in their original form, but the forest floor itself is home to more than 65,000 species of largely unstudied plants, many of them medicinal. Our logic is that the combination of shamanic intervention and the vast living pharmacopoeia of the Amazon will stack the healing odds in our favor. Plus, the warm temperatures of the jungle seem mildly less intimidating than our other leading option, the frozen steppes of the Siberian and Mongolian outback.

The core problem that we face is one of procuring the right talent. In our exploratory trips to South America, it's become quite evident that the real healers aren't the folks who hang a shingle outside their door. The people of power in these regions are tightly guarded and often only moonlight as healers, working a regular job during daylight hours.

These unorthodox, magico-religious cultures are extremely fragile, and years of oppression and persecution at the hands of powerful entities like the Roman Catholic Church have taught them how to protect their wisdom and its keepers. Healers have organic firewalls built into the community around them and must be sought out through the proper channels.

The only way you'll get in is if they want you to, or if some huge breach of trust occurs.

So far, our unpromising list of candidates consists of a few individuals whom I've met in preliminary excursions into the jungle but who are not a great fit, and a list of elders whom I've read about in books but most likely are no longer alive.

The only other lead I have comes from two random phone calls I recently received from separate friends. The first was from my childhood buddy Mark, who upon hearing about our project called to say he knew of a shaman who occasionally traveled through the United States and was supposed to be extremely powerful. He couldn't remember his name but knew it started with an *R*.

The second call was from my friend Pete, who was dating a woman who had begun to study with a medicine man in Peru named Roman. "She told me she'd be willing to make an introduction if you'd like one," Pete told me. "This guy sounds like the real deal."

I turn to my computer screen to write Mark and Pete quick follow-up e-mails and notice a web page is still up in the browser from a late-night research binge the night before. It's a simple site for a little retreat center in the Upper Amazon basin, and there's a picture of a young man staring straight into the camera. Something about this face, particularly the eyes, stopped me in my tracks last night, and I still don't know why. Written under the photograph is the man's name: Roman Hanis.

I immediately punch in Mark's Colorado phone number. He picks up, and I ask him if the name Roman Hanis rings a bell. "Yeah, that's the shaman I told you about. I knew it began with an *R*. How did you know it?"

A quick call to Pete's girlfriend, Cynthia, confirms that the man she is speaking about is the very same Roman Hanis, and it just so happens that he'll be giving a private talk in Brooklyn in a few weeks.

■ ■ ■

Two weeks later, I am in a candlelit basement in a Russian neighborhood near Coney Island, sitting on one of the cushions ringed around a man whom synchronicity seems to have led me to. He is tall and slender, with long hair pulled back and tied loosely behind his head. Perched high on the bridge of his nose are a pair of thin-rimmed glasses, framing deep eyes that are wide open but devoid of noticeable emotion as he stares at those gathered around him. He is too light-skinned and sharp-featured to be an Amazonian native.

"If you're here," he begins, looking slowly around the room, "it's most likely because you know someone who is already a part of our spirit family and has sat in our circle before. We've invited you here tonight because you have demonstrated interest in learning about the ceremonial work we do with Amazonian and Andean healing traditions. But before we bring a newcomer into a ceremony, we feel it's best to meet you beforehand and give you a download from the jungle. It is necessary for you to know the nature of this medicine and how it came to be. Please make yourself comfortable, because the talk I am about to give is long."

Roman spends the better part of the next three hours describing the origins of Amazonian shamanism and the marriage between these powerful traditions and those of the Incan lineages in the neighboring Andes mountains.

He speaks to us of his own healing journey that started with his diagnosis with advanced Crohn's disease, a severe malady of the intestinal tract, when he was in his late teens living in Moldova, a small country in Eastern Europe. After trying a variety of modern medical procedures with minimal success, the doctors told him that they would need to remove large portions of his intestine as a last resort. Refusing to undergo this invasive surgery, he began seeking out other, alternative treatments, ultimately being called to South America in his early 20s.

In a remote jungle village in Peru, he met a Huitoto shaman named Don Sinchi who was highly respected by the locals, and the elder agreed to help Roman get better. But the medicine man warned that he was about to enter one of the most trying periods of his life.

The old healer brought Roman deep into the rain forest to a little hut by a river and opened the door. "This is where you will be staying." Inside, there was nothing but a hard wooden bed and a window. Willing to do anything to get better, Roman nodded his head in agreement. "What do we do now?"

The shaman pointed into the hut and said, "This is what you do. I'll be back tomorrow."

Don Sinchi turned to go but then stopped. "I almost forgot," he said. "I need those." He pointed to Roman's backpack and possessions. Roman was skeptical and definitely didn't want to be robbed, but he was desperate and reluctant to insult the old man, so he did as he was told and handed over all his belongings.

The afternoon and evening passed, and the shaman came back the next day with some herbs for Roman to take along with a plate of cooked green plantains and quinoa.

As Don Sinchi turned to leave, Roman asked him, "What am I supposed to do now?"

"You are doing it," replied the shaman.

The shaman visited him again one morning. A few weeks had passed, and Roman had barely left his hut but to relieve his basic human needs. Don Sinchi told him that they would be doing a ceremony that night with a sacred medicine called ayahuasca.

He sat down on the steps of Roman's hut and told him a tale of a great king who once ruled benevolently over a jungle empire that encompassed the entirety of what is now the Amazon rain forest. This king was so connected to the heavens that he only needed to look at a person who was ill and he or she would be healed.

The king lived for hundreds of years, but one day he knew it was time for him to leave this plane of existence, so he bid his people farewell and told them not to worry, that he would leave them a gift after he departed that would allow them to channel his special healing gifts and connect with the gods just as he did.

He instructed them to bury his remains in a specific clearing deep in the forest, and after he left his physical body, they did exactly that. A few days later, two plants sprouted from his grave—a vine and a green, leafy plant. The native herbalists knew this was the gift, and once the plants had matured, they took cuttings from each and began to experiment with them.

This is how the sacred brew known as ayahuasca, a medicine that is thought to be the most powerful of jungle medicines, came to be.

Roman and Don Sinchi drank ayahuasca that night, and Roman spent the entire ceremony curled up in a ball, purging from both ends, the pain in his intestines flaring up violently as plant compounds moved their way through his body. There was nothing divine about this experience for him, aside from the relief he felt once it was over.

Sitting in his hut the next morning, he felt the urge to leave the place, but something inside him told him this was his only chance at getting better. So he stayed.

Three months passed. Day after day he spent in his tiny wilderness abode, with only the creatures and plants of the forest to keep him company. He was isolated in body and mind. The shaman came once or twice a day to give him food and herbal medicines, but that was it. Once or twice a week, there would be an ayahuasca ceremony, which gradually became less painful to Roman's sensitive intestinal tract. But there were still no visions or ethereal connections to a higher realm.

He was beginning to lose himself in the forest, sometimes forgetting who he was. The symptoms of his Crohn's disease, which had defined him for so long, were also beginning to subside, no longer stabbing their way into his awareness each moment.

Six months into his healing journey, he was in the middle of an ayahuasca ceremony with Don Sinchi when suddenly everything he identified as himself began to melt into the darkness around him. He panicked, clinging feebly to the final threads of his persona, until those too slipped away. Roman had become the jungle itself—every leaf, insect, and four-legged creature, radiating with luminescence and infinite creative potential. He was everything and nothing. His physical form had dissolved fully into the night, and along with it, all the pain and discomfort it held.

This was the first time Roman had ever experienced any type of vision or spiritual phenomenon during a ceremony. Until then, it had just been an ordeal of discomfort and purging, but everything shifted in this moment. He was now surrounded by light, and a female presence began to speak to him, telling him that he was healed.

He knew it was true.

He returned to his home a few months later and told his worried family what had transpired. They gently urged him to go see a doctor and have tests done immediately. The tests came back showing no signs of Crohn's disease. Roman's digestive tract was completely healthy, with no evidence of the lesions and bleeding that had plagued his gut for more than a decade.

Now, at our gathering in Brooklyn, Roman goes on to speak of how Don Sinchi invited him to come apprentice with him, now that the foreigner had passed the first threshold of shamanic preparation—healing oneself. The past decade of his life, he says, has been spent in the Peruvian outback, working with these traditions, deepening his understanding of how to use them to continue his own spiritual work and help others.

The final hour of Roman's talk is more of a warning about what the ayahuasca ceremony entails, the emotions and shadows that can arise in one's psyche, and the physical purging and dizziness that usually occur following the consumption of the jungle medicine.

He finishes his talk, and I wait until the studio is mostly cleared out before I approach him. Roman stands from his cushion, not seeing me as he dusts himself off and reaches for his bag. He looks up and his eyes brighten. "You must be Nick," he says. "Cynthia told me to expect you tonight."

"It's an honor to meet you, Roman," I say, feeling a smile overtake my face despite my efforts to maintain a professional distance. "I could tell you a story of three coincidences that led me here tonight, but somehow I don't think you would be surprised."

"I heard about this from Cynthia as well. Let's take it as a good omen that you and I were meant to meet." He smiles. "So, will you be joining us for a ceremony?"

"Just like that? I'm in?"

"I don't know what 'in' means. I'm simply asking if you would like to sit with us."

No excuses, I think. *You've got to see where this leads.*

"Sure."

■ ■ ■

December 11, 2009
Newtown, Connecticut

I'm sitting in the tiniest room of a snow-covered New England country house along with 12 other men and women. We're packed in like sardines—at the insistence of the Peruvian shaman who presides over the proceedings. The idea is for our tight circle to be so close that our knees almost touch.

Slightly claustrophobic as I am, this is not an ideal setting for me, but I'm convinced that I've experienced enough vision-inducing drugs to tread these waters with relative grace.

We all arrived around the same time, about an hour before the ceremony was scheduled to start, and other than a few casual hellos to one another, everyone has remained fairly quiet. The one thing I have picked up from the banter between a few of the women to my left is that this is a pretty advanced group whose members have sat in ceremony with Roman before. Looks like I'm the only rookie.

As we sit in a candlelit ring, Roman gives us the following words of wisdom:

You will see many things tonight, some pleasant and some not so pleasant. My advice to you is to assume a comfortable position, focus only on your breathing, and try to be still.

Proceed through the next eight hours with an open heart, an open mind, like a child does, with no attachment whatsoever to what you witness, good or bad. You will most likely feel some disturbing emotions, visions, and thoughts; don't push them away. Let them pass by, simply observing without connecting any meaning.

You also may experience some beautiful sensations and imagery. The same principle applies to these. Do not reach for them or attach any significance. Simply notice. Envision yourself as a young child, sitting on the bank of a river, watching as leaves, branches, flowers, insects, and maybe some fish float and swim past you. The child simply watches, without injecting any ego or inner assessment into these passers-by.

Stay present with all that you experience. Focus on your breathing in times of difficulty, and try not to resist or cling to what you are about to see. You are everything. You are nothing. In this way, you can fully experience Grandma and go deeper with her.

Seems simple enough.

"You each have a bucket in front of you, which you will most likely be using to purge at least one time tonight. Keep it close, and try not to confuse it with your neighbors'."

A few people chuckle at this; apparently this is something that happens. I feel the first pang of fear well up in my stomach.

The shaman produces a small flute from his bag. Perched on the edge of his cushion, he looks at everyone in the circle one by one, starting with the woman sitting immediately to his left, at 1 o'clock, and working his around to the man sitting at 11. His face is kind, but there's a graveness to his expression that activates a survival instinct in my gut. I'm at 7 o'clock, and as our eyes meet across the circle, the reality of what I've signed on for sets in.

Roman plays a short and beautiful song on his flute to commence the ceremony, as his apprentice carefully places two clear bottles containing a brownish orange substance on the floor in front of him. Once the melody is complete, he says a quiet prayer in Quechua and begins to call people up to drink their cup.

Some of us are completely meditative, holding pure space for each individual who approaches to receive the medicine. Others of us, myself included, are a little more restless. Even though the circle is small, I can't quite make out the short exchange of words between Roman and each recipient before they drink. I can, however, conclude that the beverage is not overly tasty, judging from their expressions after downing their cup, which range from a slight wince to controlled gagging.

As the man next to me, sitting at 6 o'clock, stands to get his cup, the tension in my chest rises a notch.

You got this. You've eaten mushrooms and other psychoactive compounds before. You'll be fine.

The very presence of this positive inner coach is alarming. It only comes out when I'm about to endure something awful.

Do what he said, and focus on your breathing . . .

The two finish their exchange. Not wanting to show my fear, I get up with as much grace as I have in me and maneuver toward the center of the circle in front of the cross-legged shaman.

"Hello, Nick. How are you feeling?"

"Scared."

"It's good to be afraid sometimes. Fear is not our enemy, and it often comes on the path of our own evolution. I'm happy that you are joining us tonight."

Roman unscrews the top of the one-liter plastic bottle by his knee and fills a small clay vessel roughly the size of a double shot glass. He lights a small stick of incense, known in South America as *palo santo*, and holds it over the top of the cup while he prays in an indistinguishable language with eyes closed. When his blessing is complete, he hands me the cup.

I bow and raise it to my lips with both hands. I do my best to let the thick, sticky liquid drop straight past my tongue, but the taste takes over my mouth nonetheless. A combination of bile, apricot juice, and alkaline battery, the gulp hits my stomach and immediately wants to come back up. Eyes watering, I do my best to bow again to the shaman and crawl back over to my cushion. A few minutes pass and the feeling of nausea subsides—replaced by a renewed sense of general unease.

After the final cup is administered, Roman fills it once more. He closes his eyes and prays very quietly to himself for a few moments. His eyelids open, and he raises the cup to us all and says, "*Salud,*" before downing its contents.

His face doesn't contort like the rest of ours after drinking the brew. Instead he seems to be taking in the flavor, searching with his taste buds for certain characters in the blend, almost like a wine connoisseur might let a sip linger on his or her tongue and carefully experience its effects of taste and smell.

Putting the cup down, Roman meets eyes with us once more. "Because you are my advanced group and have all sat in ceremony with me quite a few times—well, almost all of you—I have a special gift from Grandma that you are welcome to try if you feel so inclined."

The woman to his left, who is apparently one of his apprentices, pulls out an additional plastic bottle that, through the dim candlelight, seems to contain a similar substance.

"Over the past year of carrying this batch, a sediment has formed on the bottom of our jugs that is, in essence, a concentrated ayahuasca toffee. In the jungle we call it candy. This medicine is very potent, so I will only be giving one teaspoonful for those who would like to try it."

As each person in the circle approaches the shaman and is served a teaspoon, two things suddenly occur to me. One, since I am in an advanced group, this medicine is probably very strong. Two, nobody is saying no to the candy, and I won't let myself be the only one who does. Which means I'm about to double down on my ayahuasca dosage.

Moments later, I'm seated in front of Roman scraping the thick caramel jungle goo off the teaspoon with my teeth and feeling it slide with a *kerplunk* into my digestive system.

I go back to my spot in the sardine circle, fending off the urge to regurgitate, and sit down cross-legged on a cushion. We sit, letting the digestive discomfort settle, for about 30 minutes in complete silence that is broken only by the occasional whisper, waiting for the medicine to come alive within us.

In anticipation of what is about to happen, I can't help staring at the woman at 1 o'clock, who drank first, to see if there is any noticeable change in her manner or outward appearance as the ayahuasca takes hold. Nothing noticeable is happening, unless she's a total master. Eyes are still peacefully open, breathing seems normal, vomit bucket is still pristine.

Then I see it.

Starting with Ms. One O'clock, heads and bodies begin slumping, one by one, tipping like dominoes in order of who drank first. It takes only about 15 seconds for this wave of impossibility to make its way around the circle to me.

It starts as a tingle up my fingers into my arms accompanied by a loudening hum. Within moments I am enveloped by it. My strength and sensation of being in a physical form evaporates almost instantly—and it's not pretty. I'm panicking and beginning to struggle for breath. I dissolve into and through the floor, and all of my deepest fears come surging up through the darkness to greet me.

A shrill voice in me cries out that I've made a terrible mistake ingesting this unknown potion and that I'm dying. I'm tumbling through nothingness. The only remnants of the sardine circle are the distant echoes of a shaman singing his *ícaros* (ceremonial prayer songs) to the beat of a drum.

I am falling, clinging to any thought, desperately trying to get a foothold. But the only ledges and ropes offered from myself to myself are words of fear, shame, and sadness—each one building on the others.

As the storm rages on, I become keenly aware of a pressure that is starting in my bowels and bubbling up through my stomach. I'm partly relieved to be feeling my body for a moment, but this is immediately replaced by panic at this growing sensation within me. I fight it, pushing it back down with all my might. Nobody else in the circle has used a bucket, and I don't want to be the first. *At least you're still there enough to care, Nick. Maybe you're not as lost as you thought.*

And then it comes. The loudest, most ferocious vomit I've ever purged, right into my neighbor's throw-up bucket. The sound startles the entire room, and I hear my neighbor involuntarily laugh while whimpering at the intensity he's apparently in the midst of. I heave one more time, now deciding that this will be my bucket, and I lean back with a moan of my own. I hear a moan come from another spot on the circle, causing a chain of moans that bends back around to me, like one long snake working a sensation through its system.

The purge seems to have stopped my descent into the hellfire abyss momentarily. I look across the room and see the shadow that is Roman bringing an object to his chest. He plucks a stringed instrument and begins to sing a haunting song that dips and soars, changing the shape, color, and dimension of the room with each note.

"Ayahuasca, la-di-di, ayahuasca, la-di-di. Ladidididididididi-diddidi . . ."

It's too much to bear. I'm swallowed by it again.

Mid-somersault through the void, something unexpected happens. My right foot begins to ache from a recent running injury that's been nagging me for months. Just then, the first emotionally neutral thought enters my consciousness. *My foot hurts so bad right now.*

In that moment—almost as if I hit pause on the TV—the free fall stops.

I slowly open my eyes onto a whirlwind of cosmic activity happening in the darkness before me, but not in my immediate vicinity. The circle of bodies is covered in an explosion of geometric textures and images, too much for me to try and comprehend.

Looking down in the direction of my welcome foot pain, I see that my right foot is now glowing a dim blue. The pain pulses one more time. Almost instinctively I bring my left hand up to my face, and it ignites in the darkness. I place my now white hand on blue foot and watch with silent astonishment. The pain dissolves into the darkness while the white glow engulfs the foot up to the knee.

In that moment, I'm not attaching any words or emotions to the experience, simply witnessing with an empty mind what is in front of me.

But this unbroken consciousness lasts only so long, and a moment later I say a few innocent but ego-driven words to myself. *I think I've got the hang of this now.*

As if a trapdoor has opened underneath me, I fall back through the floor and into another terrifying plummet. The next few hours continue much like this, with periods of feeling lost and overwhelmed followed by moments of respite that are achieved only by stopping my ticker tape of inner self-talk.

I find that most words are "hot," meaning they trigger free fall. But certain words can be said again and again like a mantra to bridge those moments of doubt that are often accompanied by self-chatter. The battle-tested words I hear myself using most are *thank you, Grandma,* and *love.*

■　■　■

Drinking ayahuasca is like letting the forest and all the laws that govern it into your body. This medicine shows you what is really there, who you really are, what *this* really is. If you've been telling yourself stories or spackling over holes, the jig is up as soon as you enter the circle.

My mind is a constant stream of thoughts, primarily consisting of words and images. Some words are benevolent, but others carry a deeply negative charge that disturbs the harmony in my reality whenever conjured.

The power of words isn't a new idea. It's a major talking point of self-help gurus who preach positive thinking and the law of attraction (something that helped me quite a bit earlier in life). Even in popular, non-hippie-granola-eater culture, the truth of that law is recognized. As they say, the pen is mightier than the sword. But this is all vanilla compared with the loving cosmic bitch slap that Grandma gives us. At the height of ceremony, she delivers direct analytics on each word I'm thinking and the implications for the integrity of my soul.

It's grueling to be tossed around in the turbid waters of your own scattered, self-defeating, and excruciatingly potent thoughts. There are some images in the feed, but the majority of the inner dialogue, for me, is made up of words.

■ ■ ■

As the ceremony howls on, I gradually learn how to quiet my mind and let the thoughts go. At a moment of total emptiness, I begin to feel the presence of a familiar and welcome feminine entity descend upon me. The tingle of soothing warmth flooding my system is such a contrast to the deep discomfort and semi-terror I've been feeling that my eyes begin to tear and my body shudders.

Everyone talks about Grandma Ayahuasca, but I had always thought it was just another thread of rich tribal mythology. I was wrong. I am now in the presence of a feminine spirit who is communicating with me without using words. I am not looking at a woman in front of me in the dark. She is coming into my body through the top of my head and filling me up. Crazy, I know. You can't make this stuff up.

She tells me she's proud of me for facing my own fears and suffering in order to find truth. "I am with you now and will be for the rest of the night, even if you don't think I'm there." She encourages me to stay sitting up even though I'm exhausted; there is still a lot more she wants to show me.

"You may think I'm gone while you're working through a disturbance, but I promise I won't let you stray too far into the darkness. Are you ready to go deeper?"

I'm actually being offered a choice here. The volume on the suffering could actually be turned down if I ask. Just moments before, I would have done anything to make this stop—hell, I thought I was going to die. Yet the knowledge that Grandma is *real* and is with me tonight has changed everything. Emboldened by her words of encouragement, I am shocked to hear myself communicating back that I'm willing to go anywhere she takes me.

Buckle up.

I sit there in the whirling storm of the earth mother, or *Pachamama*, smelling of vomit and breathing very heavily, unable to get quite enough oxygen into my body. I begin to poke back at the beast that is me.

Somehow the quintessential negative words like *evil* and *bad* don't seem to have any effect or induce free fall. I categorize them as benign for now. The derailing thought forms are much more slithery and disarmingly normal. Something as innocent as "I can't handle any more of this" becomes an immediately self-fulfilling prophecy, intensifying the experience to the point of near unbearability. Unless I can neutralize the emotion in the next moment, all energy and equilibrium leave me and the level of visual and aural chaos gusting around me escalates as I hurtle downward out of my body into a sea of misery.

But my recovery time is improving. I find myself in this purgatory for only a few minutes at a time now, before I remember the operating principle of emptiness and acceptance. As I'm learning the hard way, holding balance in these ceremonies requires the sitter to remain thought-free, something that is far easier said than done. I realize then that the absence of thought in our culture is associated with lack of intelligence, unrealized potential, laziness—another stale concept that I am discarding as of tonight. Thoughtlessness is highly underrated.

Every twenty minutes or so, Grandma picks me up by the scruff like a pup and plops me into a new scenario, whether it's an actual change of location in place and time, or the sudden onset of a deafeningly loud *hummmmmmmm* like a thousand bees in my ears, or a challenging bodily sensation that culminates in a forceful physical purge into my handy puke bucket. About four hours into the ceremony, I'm getting used to the suffering and now understand the purpose it serves. But I am being brought closer and closer to my edge, and when I start to tailspin, the only thing that can right my vessel is stopping thought or calling on my newfound power words.

When I briefly come back to awareness of my body, I find that I'm sitting directly on the bones of my butt with my back fully erect and both hands in the air directly over my head, with palms outstretched. I'm rocking forward and backward, thanking Roman for the powerful ícaros he is singing from across the room.

"Ayahuasca, wa-di-di, ayahuasca, la-di-di. Ladididididididididididdidi . . ."

His haunting voice is not merely providing ambience for our journey with Grandma; these ancient songs were spun together by the masters to bring everyone deeper into their intensity and strengthen the effects of the medicine. In one moment, the music can be torturously needling to the psyche and nerves, but then in another, when all seems lost, it can actually help you find your way back.

Right now, I am making what appears to be a physical gesture of gratitude and humility to Roman, who sits somewhere in front of me in the hot blackness. Am I really grateful, or am I striking this pose of gratitude to counter the disturbing feelings that his words are invoking inside me? I don't know, but questioning anything I'm doing in the moment is a total no-no, if I want to stay above decks.

■ ■ ■

After about four hours of learning how to stay afloat and right the canoe when it capsizes, I notice a very clear visual metaphor emerging. Inside me—not in my body, but inside *me*—there is a large pendulum, sitting relatively motionless at this current moment. To its right live joy, elation, excitement, bliss, beauty, and ecstasy. On the path of its leftward swing live fear, sadness, grief, shame, and despair.

It seems pretty obvious that the right side of the long pendulum arm is where the preferred experiences are, and for the first few hours tonight, those were what I was reaching for, chasing after the appealing visions and emotions that flashed across my ticker tape while fighting to keep the more disturbing apparitions and emotions at bay.

But a pendulum, by its very nature, swings. As I cling to positive sensations, I'm in effect pulling my pendulum from its center, drawing it against the cosmic gravity by which it operates, cocking it back like the hammer of a revolver so that even the slightest slip of the finger will send it crashing down, swooping through and past center into the opposite realm. The realm of suffering and disorientation.

Similarly, when I indulge the resulting panic and despair with even more defeating thoughts and word forms (*Oh, shit! I'm going to die!* or my new favorite, *You pushed it too far this time. You'll never make it back. You're not strong enough to handle this. Roman and the others are going to know you're a phony now*), I push the pendulum even deeper into that dark frontier. Now the slightest glimpse of comfort or hope will send it crashing back the other way, past center again, surging into the ecstasy that awaits on the other side.

The result is a roller-coaster ride that many experience in the stronger ceremonies—not only with ayahuasca, but with *any* ancient rite of passage. These spiritual interventions are all about the same thing—bringing individuals into full contact with their fear, their mortality, and ultimately their power. This is usually done via intentional intensity, whether that be the heat of a sweat lodge, the physical trial of a sun dance, or the consumption of a psychoactive substance like ayahuasca, peyote, San Pedro cactus, mushroom, or venom.

After tonight, I will use the pendulum as an operating principle for ceremonies and life itself. Keep that arm still—always.

■ ■ ■

By four in the morning, our circle has lost its shape, morphing into a scattering of bodies in varying states of consciousness. Some are still in the throes of Grandma's teachings, sighing and whimpering now and then; others are in deep sleep, unbothered by the lack of proper bedding. The room has become something akin to a hive, one writhing pile of bodies curled up with little concern about the proximity of others.

We've been through something together. The shared suffering and the space we've held for one another's vulnerability have forged a primal bond among us all. The notion of social awkwardness is thousands of miles away from us now. My elbow is touching another's woman's foot, and part of my blanket is being used by my neighbor to the left. The room has become one living, breathing organism.

■ ■ ■

My head is still humming as I walk down the stairs of the contemporary, modern home into the living room. It's been only a few hours since Roman officially closed the ceremony with a prayer and a song he played on a crooked instrument resembling a dwarf guitar. The sun has just started to rise, and the little den behind me is full of slumbering bodies. I'm too awake to sleep.

Reality has changed. Everything I thought I was, everything I thought *this* was, is so much simpler now. But within that simplicity is an infinite space that feels like home.

All the stories about Nick are gone. There's been a purification, and all that remains is the essential me. And this essential me is thirsty.

Weaving and bobbing on unsteady legs, I make my way through the living room in the direction of what I'm hoping will be the kitchen. From around the corner I hear the chopping of knife on cutting board and quiet, lighthearted banter. I enter the kitchen and see two women busily chopping garlic and squeezing lemons at the counter. Any trepidation I might have felt the night before at the thought of walking into a conversation between two strangers is completely absent at the present moment.

"Hi. I'm Nick. I think. Actually, I'm not sure who I am anymore." This prompts us all to laugh, and one of them comes over and gives me a big, loving hug.

"My name is Erica," she says. "I was sitting next to you last night, remember?"

I get another hug from the other woman. "I'm Sara."

Standing there, I'm struck by the fact that these two people seem like sisters to me now. I'm not used to being embraced by someone so intimately without some kind of sexual connotation. Yet it's not there.

There is a comradery and a clarity among us. Maybe it's because we three stepped over the edge together last night and faced our deepest, darkest terrors while purging our systems of everything toxic—physical, mental, emotional, and spiritual. But there's more to it than that.

"Here. Have some lemon and garlic water. It will settle your stomach." Sara slides a freshly poured glass in my direction. It seems like the last thing my raw digestive tract would want right now, but I do as I'm told. As the bitter juice and chunks of garlic hit my stomach, the effect is not what I expected. The mixture actually settles my remaining queasiness and grounds my feet to the floor.

The three of us sit down and begin to share our experiences from the ceremony. I'm struck by how different our journeys were. I assumed that everyone in the circle was in free fall with me for half the night, but each of us has had a remarkably unique and intricate encounter with the medicine. More people trickle into the kitchen with the same kindred demeanor, exchanging hugs and grabbing a cup of the lemon and garlic elixir.

I haven't known these people for more than 12 hours, yet they are seeing me in the most open and honest state I've ever known. A bond has formed within our gang of survivors. We are a spirit family.

∎ ∎ ∎

A few hours later, I'm sitting on the stone hearth of a warm fire-place, connecting with a few of the men and women from the ceremony, when I hear my name called from another room.

"Nick, come with me." It's Roman.

I walk into the kitchen and over to the back door, where I see him waiting.

"I want to show you something." With that, he turns the knob and pushes open the door, carving an arc-shaped path in the thick snow outside. He remains in the doorway as the freezing winter air rushes into the cozy house. "Take off all of your clothes," he says.

"What?" That is the last thing on earth I want to do.

Roman looks up at me as he takes his own shoes and pants off. "Believe me. This will be good for you."

I reluctantly do as he says, and out we walk, bare feet disappearing into about 12 inches of frozen powder with each step. My survival instincts kick into high gear as the skin on my feet, ankles, and calves is engulfed in white. We can't possibly last out here for more than a minute. I grew up in these parts and know that frostbite is a very dangerous thing to mess around with.

Not wanting to "fail" this test of spiritual fortitude, I involuntarily begin to hunch and hug myself. Roman stops in his tracks and turns to face me in the yard. He sees what I'm doing and his face breaks into a wide, childlike grin.

"We think we're so frail, don't we? Raised with so much fear. It wasn't always this way." He is standing casually, as if we were still inside the warm kitchen rather than out in the bitter cold. "Put the strongest man or woman out in the cold for a few moments, and they become overwhelmed with an urge to tense up, as though that will somehow keep the cold out. But if you can do the unthinkable and let the sensation flow into and through you—observing it without emotion or fear, letting it pass—your reality is transformed."

As he speaks, the biting cold that is assaulting me from every angle begins to transform into something different.

Information.

A natural self-scanning mechanism begins, showing me where I'm blocked, where I need to let go.

"Your body knows what it needs to maintain equilibrium. Don't let your mind get in the way."

As he's talking, my eyes begin to move to the tall and equally naked trees that loom up around us. In the dead of winter, everything is silent. But as we stand there, I begin to hear the birch and the pine. With each subtle creak and groan of living trees, my body becomes less shaky. The needling prickles of cold snow and winter air on my flesh melt away.

"Ah, he's connecting with the trees," Roman says to himself (or someone I can't see). "Let's walk."

I nod, as if the idea of walking through an arctic landscape completely naked is old hat to me. Off we go, trekking through the woods, listening to the trees, rocks, and wind. Thirty minutes later we're still alive and plodding our way over a rock wall toward a large frozen pond.

Without communicating a word, he and I break into a run toward the ice. Two full-grown men, completely naked, ice-skating on bare feet in 15-degree cold, laughing like giddy children. The air and snow feel cold but refreshing.

"How long can we stay out here without dying?" I ask.

"You already died last night! No need to worry about that anymore. Just keep focusing on your breath. The breath is the only possession that we need in this life."

Thirty minutes later, as we casually approach the house in the final light of day, a thought crosses my mind. *Either this was a huge spiritual opening, or I've gone mad and will need to have my toes amputated.*

Before opening the door, Roman turns to me and says, "Okay. I think we can do this movie together."

Sitting in the warm kitchen a few moments later, I'm startled to see that my feet and calves (which had been submerged in snow for more than 60 minutes) aren't even red. A warm bowl of soup is slid over to me across the kitchen counter as I put my clothes back on.

Roman's words suddenly sink in. We're actually going to be making this documentary.

THE HEALING POWER OF FIRE AND ICE

From the bathhouses of Europe to Native American sweat lodges, people have been using hot and cold to purify both body and spirit for millennia. In Mayan culture, a steam bath called a temazcal is used, like a sweat lodge, to detoxify the body during sickness, to connect to higher realms, and as a sacred place for women to give birth.

Controlled exposure to hot and cold environments has many scientifically proven health benefits. It increases blood circulation, flushes toxins, and kills bacteria and viruses that can't survive at certain temperatures.

It's interesting to note that indigenous cultures from opposite sides of the planet utilize very similar hot/cold techniques for health and wellness. Is it an innate understanding in us humans?

Similar to the Mayan temazcal, the Russian banya is a small bathhouse, usually situated near a source of ice-cold water. This structure is used to harness the health benefits of intentional temperature variation. Found all over Eastern Europe, banyas often contain branches of fresh or dried leaves or herbs for bathers to hit or massage themselves with, further improving circulation, much like the bundles of herbs used by the Maya in Honduras, Guatemala, and Mexico.

As with a temazcal or a traditional sweat lodge, participants in a banya come together to heal and purify in a communal setting. It's customary to take breaks in between sessions in a banya, during which bathers often cool off in a cold lake or roll around in the snow.

The cycle of hot and cold is repeated in order to achieve the maximum health benefit.

Cold on its own has been used as a means of healing since the ancient Egyptians, who recognized that cold can minimize pain and reduce inflammation. The ancient Greeks regularly bathed in cold water with the belief that it improved their vigor. Hippocrates, often referred to as the father of modern medicine, recommended a regimen of alternating temperatures, switching between hot and cold baths, to improve circulation and digestion. While heat relaxes, cold stimulates, and both can be utilized for healing.

In addition to the many proven health benefits of hot and cold therapies, ancient peoples also understood these rituals to be medicine for the mind, spirit, and heart. Across cultures, the aim of hot and cold rituals is purification. The sweat lodge, temazcal, banya, and bathhouse serve as a sacred refuge where we can release physical, emotional, and spiritual toxicity.

There is nothing I know of that awakens the soul like a hot steam followed by a plunge into ice-cold water or snow. I think Hippocrates might agree!

Although the examples I've shared here are specific to their regions, you can find ways to use hot and cold therapy in your own bathroom. It can be something as simple as aiming your showerhead (even better if it's handheld) at a spot where you have aches and pain or tenseness and switching between hot and cold water every 30 seconds; just be careful with sensitive areas like the face and neck.

We need to be a little adventurous to evolve and grow.

Chapter 4

<><><><><><><><><><><>

THE WALL

Security is mostly a superstition. It does not exist in nature,
nor do the children of men as a whole experience it. Avoiding
danger is no safer in the long run than outright exposure.
Life is either a daring adventure, or nothing.

—HELEN KELLER

July 7, 2010
Denver, Colorado

The team and I are staring at The Wall.

Three weeks ago, we sent out an e-mail to the online communities from our past documentaries announcing that our next healing film would be taking place in the Amazon rain forest.

If you know someone who is suffering from a serious illness
and would be interested in putting the natural herbs and cere-
monies of South American shamans to the test, please complete
the attached application. We cannot guarantee a cure, but we
are very optimistic that this region holds plants and protocols
that the Western world is not yet aware of.

We wanted to make sure that only serious individuals responded, so the remainder of the message was a fire-and-brimstone list of the many dangers and potential hardships that applicants might encounter on a jungle trip like this. While venturing to the tropical frontier of Peru wouldn't take us out of the Western Hemisphere, it would certainly take us beyond the safety and comfort of the modern, industrialized West. We hoped to get two or three good candidates this way, which would be a great start.

Forty-eight hours later, we're looking at more than 400 applications from people around the world, men and women who have been failed by modern medicine and are looking for new answers to their illnesses—breast cancer, Parkinson's disease, AIDS, M.S., diabetes, depression, addiction, PTSD. Many of them are difficult to read because of the sheer desperation that is conveyed in the applicants' words.

Some people are writing excitedly, having heard about the promising undiscovered herb medicines of the Amazon, but others are simply reaching for any inkling of hope.

We're only going to be able to take eight.

Do all of these people really understand what they are signing up for? To make sure they do, I send out another gut-check e-mail to all applicants reiterating the extreme conditions they will face if they are one of the eight patients selected. Poisonous snakes, poisonous spiders, 100 percent humidity, complete solitary confinement in their own rustic jungle hut, no electricity, no modern plumbing, thousands of miles away from a modern medical facility, an infinite number of mosquitoes . . . Plus, we will be filming their entire experience—the good, the bad, and the ugly.

For better or worse, this cuts the list of applicants in half. Now we're looking at 200 people who are willing to brave anything for a shot at a cure. We call each of these folks personally to get a better idea of their personality and make sure they are comfortable with the psychoactive plants that are used in some of the healing ceremonies. This whittles our list of 200 down to the grid of 100 remaining candidates adorning The Wall.

Dan, Michelle, and I stand in front of that wall for the better part of two days debating who are the best fits. There's so much to consider: Do we want to stick to outdoorsy people who we know can handle the experience, or would it be best to select people who will be challenged by the elements? Should we say yes to people with late-stage cancer and advanced Parkinson's, or would it be wisest to stick with patients who do not have potentially terminal conditions? Every hour, The Wall gets more complex. It is beginning to resemble a murder board on a TV crime show.

It's early evening when we finally come to our senses and realize there's no way we can make a decision before Roman weighs in.

I send Roman a quick e-mail, hoping he is at his part-time apartment in the jungle port city of Iquitos. He's been busy making preparations on the other side of the equator, essentially overseeing the construction of a rudimentary Amazonian healing center that will serve as the setting for our living experiment. He's been calling me weekly from one of the few Internet cafés in the entire province with decent enough bandwidth to place a Skype call—and it's still patchy. As of our last conversation, half of the structures had been erected by a team of locals on a remote plot of jungle about an hour's drive into the bush.

We hear back from Roman within an hour. Moments later, the three of us are sitting around a laptop in my kitchen, speaking to him over a choppy Skype call.

Roman initially feels that we should choose eight patients with somewhat less serious conditions, like diabetes, depression, and addiction. He thinks it would be best to work with people who will be able to maneuver more easily in the jungle and who are not at risk of dying from their illness during the monthlong healing journey.

I look at Dan and Michelle. "I understand your point, Roman, but I think it would be a good idea to read you some of these other applications."

We spend the next 15 minutes reviewing a small group of profiles from some of our more desperate patients that really call out to us. I share some of my personal conversations with them and find myself advocating for a few in particular. They know this is their last shot and are going into this with a full understanding of what it could mean. The ayahuasca ceremonies themselves might be a powerful way for terminally ill patients to get a peek behind the curtain and process any fears around mortality. If it doesn't heal them, it could very likely give them a glimpse of where they are going once they make their final transition.

By the end of the night, we finally agree on eight patients who have a combination of health conditions: three people with cancer (stage 4 breast cancer, stage 4 neuroendocrine cancer, and stage 2 prostate cancer), a woman with Parkinson's disease, a woman with Crohn's, a woman with IBS, a man with depression and addiction, and a man with type 2 diabetes.

Garry, Melinda, John, Nicola, Jessica, Gretchen, Juan, and Joel. Eight people with eight different illnesses, who have each assured us that they are ready to do anything it takes to heal.

I'll be calling each of them over the next 24 hours to give them the good news, but I still don't think they have any idea what lies in store for them in two months.

No turning back now.

■　■　■

Iquitos, Peru
July 28, 2010

Michelle and I are in the back of a mototaxi—a sort of motorcycle-enabled rickshaw—bobbing and weaving through the crowded streets of the Amazonian port city of Iquitos, on our way to meet Roman.

We're only two months away from the main event, and the purpose of this final preparatory journey is to meet two more shamans who we hope will be joining us for the monthlong retreat. That will make three shamans, one modern doctor, and two nurses, the goal being to bring in both ancestral healing strategy and sound medical oversight.

Most of the mototaxis in this region are imported from Southeast Asia and India for their versatility on dirt roads and city pavement, but the suspension on these things is minimal or missing altogether. We take a corner a little too sharply and thump hard, hanging on with arms hooked over a crossbar to keep our heads from knocking together.

The driver has a sleek build and dark skin that is characteristic of the local Shipibo Connibo tribe. As we putt down the broken cobblestone road, he turns around, sizes me up with a charming smile, and asks in Spanish, "Are you headed into the jungle to drink ayahuasca?"

"Wow. Is it that obvious, or do you say that to all the foreigners?"

Seemingly impressed that I can at least speak Spanish, he takes his attention off the uneven road—longer than I'm comfortable with on a crowded street—to face me once more. His playful eyes become grave as he says, "A little warning, my friend. Grandmother Ayahuasca is very powerful, but the forests themselves are even stronger medicine. Many come to this region to find shamans, but they soon realize that the jungle itself is a fierce spirit, more potent than any herbal concoction."

Those scary trees in *The Wizard of Oz* that attack Dorothy with apples immediately come to mind.

"It gets into your blood," the driver continues. "It comes calling for you."

This isn't the first time I've heard far-out native legends about *la selva* (the jungle), and I do what I always do—listen respectfully and thank the man for his insight. There are so many old wives' tales and bits of ancestral mythology that need to be navigated in these cultures—some hold real, practical application, like burning disinfectant tree resin to clear the air of germs, but others feel like something out of a fairy tale.

We reach our destination, a beat-up red van against which Roman is leaning casually. I hop out of the mototaxi and thank the driver, handing him a few extra *soles*. I don't know it now, but his words of wisdom will become a core part of my personal survival protocol for the next few months.

. . .

I snap awake in the darkness, unable to breathe. I can't see anything, and the blackness that surrounds my body is screaming with thousands of little voices, a storm of alien sounds.

Gasping for air, I don't know where—or, more alarmingly, *who*—I am. In a terrified frenzy, I scramble to my feet and become entangled in some kind of spiderweb, then stumble over objects underfoot in the general direction of anything that might help me.

Air is filling my lungs, but no relief is coming. I need to stop this sound before my heart explodes . . .

My hand finds a door handle and I pull it. Walking outside, I stare up and see the first familiar sight—the night sky, sparkling with stars. My heart begins to calm and the air comes easier. As the unrelenting sea of noise continues to rage on around me, I begin to remember who I am.

This body belongs to someone named Nick, and the wall of babbling screams belongs to the millions of insects, reptiles, and tree-dwelling mammals that live here in the Amazon rain forest, which is where "I" am.

Nick is currently experiencing the sanity-threatening essence of this place. It won't let him go. The jungle, once it has you in its grip, is like a marathon you can't stop running. On nights like these, I lose my ability to differentiate myself from the raging spiritscape that engulfs me. I know this is helping me purify in a real and meaningful way, but these dissociative episodes are terrifying.

The jungle itself is medicine, my friend. You will soon realize that. The Peruvian in the mototaxi was right.

Once I'm firmly reintegrated into the human suit that is Nick, I make my way back to the thatch-roofed longhouse I'm bunking in with my film team. Creeping over the hand-hewn wood floor, I crawl back under my mosquito net (not a spiderweb after all) and find Michelle waiting for me.

"Where were you? Did it happen again?" She speaks softly, but her voice is loud enough to be heard through the high-decibel organic static that surrounds us.

"Yeah. I'm fucking scared."

"Come here." She pulls me closer and puts my head on her belly. "Just breathe. I'm right here."

In the weeks since we arrived, Michelle has transformed dramatically, from a late-20s, cosmopolitan socialite to a fully realized earth mama. This effect seems to be taking hold of a few of the other women who came with us as well. The womblike nature of this place is unlocking a way of being in them that is humbling to watch.

I am going through a rebirthing process of my own, but it's shaking the core of who I am. Stepping into this place is like stepping into a living bath of truth serum. Every belief you have about yourself is pressure-tested, weighed and measured, and put on the existential chopping block. The ceremonial work we are doing with plant medicines like ayahuasca and the mescaline cactus known as San Pedro are extremely powerful, but just living in this intense environment is equally revelatory. I feel like I'm being unraveled, realization by realization. The stories I've told myself and others about who I am and what *this* is are starting to seem alarmingly thin.

The good news is that one very vital piece of my identity has remained fairly intact throughout this trial by fire. I've made a few refinements, but my intention and stated life purpose still seem pretty sturdy, even after being run through the mill on a nightly basis.

My job in this incarnation is to be a bridge between the new ways and the old in whatever capacity I see that serves the greater good. I have always had a knack for winning people's trust, and it appears I am also sensitive to subtle energies. I now understand that I must use those skills to bring the ancient healing knowledge of the tribes forward to those who are suffering, while at the same time awakening the modern world to the importance of preserving these fast-disappearing traditions and the vital wisdom they hold.

The rest of the stories about Nick and his life are falling away very quickly, and the gaps left by these deleted passages are quite possibly causing the terrifying disconnections between mind and body that I'm experiencing on nights like these. Hopefully these are temporary blanks that are just waiting to be rewoven into a cohesive fabric. Only time will tell.

Roman always advises his patients that a three-month period of integration is needed after each major threshold is crossed on the healing path. I realize now that I've been subconsciously dismissing this shamanic recommendation as more mere symbolism from Amazonian lore, and not an actual prescription.

The same way I dismissed the mototaxi driver's words about the jungle.

What else haven't I been fully hearing?

■   ■   ■

The following night, Roman invites us to sit in an ayahuasca ceremony with a small group of people, including two other shamans, Edwin and Habin. Roman has asked them to be present so I can get a feel for their energy and consider involving them in our upcoming retreat. We're sitting on a concrete slab in the basement of a newly constructed longhouse with 13 other patients and seekers in addition to the three shamans.

These two new shamans are complete opposites, visually speaking. Edwin has the dark complexion and short, stout frame of the locals, while Habin's pale skin and lankiness bespeak a European bloodline.

The three maestros are spaced intentionally around the circle, positioned to create an equilateral triangle between them. Each one has a mesa blanket—a handwoven prayer mat from this region—laid out before them with their personal power objects and healing tools (crystals, statuettes, palo santo wood, bottles of flower essence, dried herb bundles) resting on top. I don't know whether to be reassured or intimidated by this unusually low participant to shaman ratio—the ceremony is usually led by only one.

Turn the thoughts off, Nick.

Once we've drunk and the candles are blown out, Roman asks Habin to sing an opening ícaro, a song of prayer that is sung during ayahuasca ceremonies. The pale shaman's voice grumbles to life in the darkness, rolling through the room in a melodic hybrid of Spanish and Quechua. Whoever this man is, he has lived in these parts for a very long time.

A few hours later, the ceremony is fully alive and our circle is pulsing, each participant on his or her own cosmic journey.

Suddenly a shrill sound creeps into the room, and Roman, who is mid-ícaro, stops singing at once. Silence. Everyone in the room seems to sober as we wait to hear it again.

It happens a second time, and our collective attention turns toward a woman across the circle who is curled over into the fetal position. She is rambling to herself in deep and low tones, giggling and occasionally squealing in response to something that only she can see.

Roman's voice sounds out in the night. "Habin, please see to Diana."

Habin stands up, walks over to her, puts one hand on her arm, and says something inaudible to the rest of us. She immediately sits right back up and begins to breathe normally again.

Roman asks her if she is okay, and Diana, who just moments ago was trapped in her own frightening world, responds calmly and gratefully. "Yes, Roman. Thank you for helping me, Habin. I'm okay now."

I've never seen anything like this in ceremony before. Habin did something that pulled her out of the darkness and back into the room with us.

The next morning, as we do our customary post-ceremony share circle, Diana is candid about the inner turmoil she was wrestling through.

"I don't tell many people this, but I had a twin sister who lived inside my mother's belly with me before I was born. But only I survived. And all through my childhood, whenever my lost twin sister was mentioned, my mother would always say, very casually, that she would have lived if I hadn't eaten all of her food. 'Diana, you were just a hungry baby and didn't leave enough for her.'

"All my life, I've just quietly kept this guilt inside me. I never talk about it with anyone. Then last night, after drinking Grandma, I was taken back into my mother's uterus and found my twin sister waiting for me there. It was too much for me to live through at first, and then she communicated with me that she didn't die, she joined with me in this body, this consciousness. We became one."

Diana looks at Habin with tears in her eyes and thanks him once again. The shaman gives a slight nod, his face remaining unchanged as he says, in a thick accent, "Welcome."

I decide right then that Habin is a yes for the documentary. Not only has he shown his gifts during ceremony, but he is also known in this region to be a miracle worker for certain neurological disorders. It's very common for a shaman or healer to specialize in particular illnesses of which they have an innate awareness. Habin might be a perfect match for Nicola's Parkinson's.

■ ■ ■

Two days after the ayahuasca ceremony with the three shamans, I am invited to a party to celebrate the 70th birthday of Edwin's mother at her home in a neighborhood on the outskirts of Iquitos. Roman tells me I should definitely go.

Edwin comes from a family of healers known for their expansive knowledge of jungle plant medicines. With more than 65,000 species of plants in the Amazon, of which less than 3 percent have been studied, this skill has made Edwin's family quite well known in and around Iquitos.

Later that afternoon, I hug Michelle goodbye and follow Edwin out of the center and down a path to the only road that traverses these parts. Every once in a while, a truck or mototaxi will come rumbling down the road, already loaded with locals catching a lift into town. We wait by the side of the road for about 15 minutes before we finally see an old pickup truck approaching in the direction we're headed.

The shaman flags the truck down, and the driver pulls over and waves us in. We hop in the back, introduce ourselves to the three locals who are sitting with their backs against the cab, and off we go.

Hitchhiking is the Uber of the Amazon.

An hour later, we're on the very outskirts of Iquitos, in a sea of simple one-room houses whose crumbling walls are coated with graffiti and hand-painted advertisements. Edwin slaps his hand a few times on the top of the cab to let the driver know that this is our stop.

We slide to the ground next to the pickup and hail a mototaxi. Edwin gives the driver an address, and off we go, deeper into the maze of makeshift abodes down a narrow dirt road pocked with huge puddles and potholes.

It's almost completely dark when our jungle buggy comes to a stop and Edwin nudges my arm to let me know we're here.

"Su lugar está allí," he tells me. Her place is over there. Edwin knows next to no English, just Spanish and Quechua. Hopefully the communication over the next few hours won't get too complex.

If I'm being honest with myself, this is a neighborhood I would never venture into on my own. The folks in their doorways seem extremely nice, but there's a cultural context here that I'd be a fool to ignore.

We walk down a dimly lit alleyway and begin to hear the sound of festive music. A moment later we are standing in an open doorway looking in on a huge room exploding with color and people.

The concrete floor and retractable front wall of this structure give it the feel of a big two-car garage. On the wall to the far left is an ornate shrine glowing with strings of lights and flickering candles and featuring the Virgin Mary in the place of honor.

Against the adjacent wall is a six-piece band playing an upbeat salsa tune, the lead singer belting out lyrics about the jungle, God, and walking the right path.

The middle of the room is filled with people of all ages dancing in semi-unison, smiling and laughing as they go.

When Edwin and I walk in, half the room swarms toward us—or, more accurately, toward Edwin—to say hello and give him a hug. A woman who must be his mother comes over and embraces her son, looking over at me as she does.

"This is Nick, the filmmaker I was telling you about," Edwin says.

Edwin's mother looks at me somewhat skeptically. "Why don't I get you both something to drink while Edwin introduces you to our family and friends?" She doesn't wait for a response, but turns and disappears into the crowd.

One of Edwin's sisters appears from behind us and introduces herself to me with a kind smile. "Edwin, can I talk with you for a second?" Edwin tells me he'll be right back and steps outside.

My eyes dart around the room as I contemplate my next maneuver in this lively but completely foreign social environment. Two children in front of me are dancing their pants off to the jungle jam, and they wave me over to join them, I begin toward them but stop when I feel a hand lightly take my elbow.

"Señor, you are Edwin's friend?" I turn to see a stocky older fellow looking up at me.

"Yes, I am. My name is Nick. Edwin and I have been working with some plant medicines together."

"Ah, that's a wonderful thing," says the man. "My name is Ernesto. I know Edwin well. He is a master *vegetalista.*"

"Really?" I say, hoping Ernesto will elaborate. A vegetalista is a specific title here in the jungle that refers to a healer who draws power from the plants in the region—and as any ethnobotanist worth his or her salt will tell you, only the locals know which ones do what. Although Roman and Habin are very knowledgeable about Amazonian flora, neither professes to have a true expertise in the area.

"Half the people in this room have been healed by his herbs—including me!" Ernesto taps his chest proudly and smiles. "Three years ago, I had terrible ulcers in my stomach. The clinic in Iquitos prescribed me medications, but nothing worked. One day my wife told me to go ask Rosa's son because he had the same gift as his father. I went to see Edwin, who welcomed me into his house. He examined me for an hour and then told me to come back the following day, that he was going to find the plants I needed in the jungle and prepare me a tea to drink.

"I knew he meant well," Ernesto confides, "but to be honest, I didn't think he would be able to cure me. I was wrong. I returned the next day and he had the tea ready for me. He told me to drink one cup in the morning before breakfast and one cup in the evening before dinner. I did as he said, and a week later my pain was completely gone! Many people in this room will tell you a similar story."

A tingle goes up my spine as I listen to the man speak. He then takes me by the elbow and guides me through the crowd to a wall lined with chairs, all of which are occupied by friends and family. A middle-aged woman with a bright flower in her curly hair smiles up at Ernesto and me as we approach.

"Nick," says Ernesto, "this is Maria. Maria, this is Nick, Edwin's herbalist friend." I don't have time to tell Maria I'm not actually an herbalist before she thrusts her hands toward me.

"I owe him these," she says jubilantly. "He cured my arthritis with one of his leaf wraps. I never thought I would be able to braid my granddaughter's hair again."

"That's wonderful! What type of leaves did he use?" I ask.

She looks at Ernesto quizzically. There is a translation problem, and I'm not sure whether it's my Spanish or hers that's more to blame. Ernesto repeats my question for her in Quechua, and she nods.

"It's a plant called Santa Maria," she says. "I had never heard of it until Edwin brought it to me—there are so many herbs in the forest."

I feel the tug on my elbow again, and Ernesto is once more guiding me down the line of chairs to talk to someone who I assume to be another of Edwin's patients.

But Edwin's mother intercepts us, carrying two bottles of Inca Kola (the official soft drink of Peru). "I was just looking for you, Rosa," Ernesto cries. "Tell Nick how Edwin cured your cancer."

The 70-year-old matron scowls at the old man and hands me an Inca Kola. "Have you been sharing everybody's personal health histories with our guest?" But her scowl gives way to a cautious smile as she considers me for a moment. "I would not be here if it weren't for my son," she says at last, her voice soft and her face grave. "I was on my deathbed with cancer of the colon when he was just a young man. He wasn't yet the respected vegetalista that he is now, but I knew he had his father's abilities. When the doctors said there was nothing they could do, he began to bring me medicine from the forest. The cancer was gone a few months later."

My follow-up questions to Señora Huani are drowned out when the band cranks up the amplification on its already earsplitting sound system. Finally the three of us give up on our conversation and just stand smiling politely at one another for a few moments. Then, apparently seeing no end to the loud music in sight, the others give in to the insistence of the band to join in a folk dance that everyone seems to know—except me.

I sneak outside. I need some time to think. Unless all the people in this neighborhood are conspiring, it looks like Edwin is the real deal.

So now there are three—three proven shamans from three distinct disciplines who are willing to sign on to our monthlong retreat. Edwin is about to become our resident vegetalista, master of herbs.

SHAMAN OR CHARLATAN?

Awareness of shamanic rites in the so-called Western world is growing, and one unintended by-product is a wave of pretenders, both indigenous and foreign, who call themselves shamans. The reach of capitalism knows no bounds, and the mass influx of spiritual tourism into developing countries makes fakery a tempting racket for both cash-needy locals and enterprising expats.

Many of the interventions used by shamans are intense, whether a psychoactive plant brew, a piping-hot sweat lodge, or a long period of fasting. It's important to know a healer is legit before putting your life in his or her hands. This raises an important question:

How do you spot a real shaman?

There is no cut-and-dried way to do this, but there is a short list of criteria that I use in my own travels to stay safe and save time.

When I first went to Peru, I half expected the shamans to wear unique tribal garb or some sort of sacred bling that set them apart. I was wrong. Expect a baseball cap, a T-shirt with a major brand logo on it, and a pair of cargo shorts. Yes, there are exceptions, but healers around the world look and dress the same as everyone else. Steer clear of healers who go out of their way to be noticed—flamboyance is at odds with the spirit path they espouse.

Most healers don't advertise—you have to work a bit to find them.

The majority of the world's healers work mainly within their family and local community and often have full-time jobs doing something else entirely. Their gift is often kept very private, and satisfied patients are sometimes far more vocal about it than the shamans themselves.

You saw a hint of this with Edwin's family in the preceding chapter, which I hope paints a good picture of how a healer can be vetted—by asking them and their past clients a number of questions.

What is their attitude about money?

Shamanism is one of the oldest professions known to man, and money is commonly exchanged for the services of an indigenous healer. But the energy and demeanor of the shaman in conducting this spiritual business transaction can vary drastically.

A shaman or group of shamans who are insistent and over-eager to be paid up front, for example, is a red flag straight out of the gate. Most of the bona fide healers whom we work with are concerned less about the money and more about the fit of patient to shaman. Often the payment arrangement is flexible, with fees set on a sliding scale according to what the individual can afford.

Trust your gut.

It doesn't matter how well-recommended a shaman is. If you get a not-so-fresh feeling upon meeting him or her, turn around and walk the other way. This goes for folk healers anywhere in the world. Ancestral medicine is strongly spiritual, and your intuition is going to be your best friend every step of the way, from getting to the root of an illness to homing in on the right maestro to guide you on your journey. A true shaman will respect your feeling that the energy between you is not right and your decision to continue looking until you find the right match.

Chapter 5

◇◇◇◇◇◇◇◇◇◇◇◇◇

ARRIVAL

From a certain point onward there is no longer any turning back. That is the point that must be reached.

—FRANZ KAFKA

October 15, 2010
Loreto Province, Peru

Rain. Mud. Wind.

It's the rainy season here, and the rain forest is living up to its name. Every morning we wake to a torrential downpour followed by moments of sun and clouds, and then another downpour. Everything is damp, including our bedding, clothes, and selves.

The crew and I arrived a few days ago to make final preparations with shamans and staff at the healing center before patient arrival. We've added two more specialists to our production team: Alberto, a sound technician originally from Paraguay, and a talented cameraman from New York City named Brock, whom Michelle and I have known for a long time. There are now five of us—Dan, Michelle, Brock, Alberto, and me. Only time will tell if we are fit for the task that lies ahead.

We're now only 24 hours away from the start of our Amazonian healing experiment, and the afternoon is a blur of frenzied activity: prepping the support staff with everything they need to help the patients and their unique conditions and challenges; assembling patient-specific meal plans; clearing the narrow jungle paths to each hut so those with more advanced impairments can navigate their way to and from the showering area; making sure our satellite phone, walkie-talkies, mini solar panels, and other modern devices are functioning properly.

I've never met a camera that gets along with water, and keeping our four rigs and assorted production equipment dry over the next month is going to be tricky. The weight and potential risk of what we are about to undertake is becoming more real by the moment.

When the sun goes down the night before patient arrival, the film team and staff members have a long debriefing, led by Roman and me. We spend this final powwow going over "what if" scenarios, of which there are an infinite number. The four women (two nurses and two attendants) who are in charge of day-to-day patient care ask a number of questions, voicing emergency-oriented concerns like "What do we do in the event of a snake or spider bite?" as well as more practical ones like "What do we do if a patient demands a food that is counter to the jungle diet he or she is prescribed? How firm a stance should we take?"

"They are here to heal," Roman tells them. "They all know what they signed up for. This is not Club Med, and the diet is not optional."

He looks at everyone on the staff to make sure his words are perfectly understood. It's not my place to argue, and I wouldn't if it were. As Roman said in his pre-ceremony talk in Brooklyn last year, Don Sinchi healed him of severe Crohn's disease using an extremely strict protocol—seclusion in a jungle hut, basic food for sustenance only, herbal formulas, and weekly ceremonies.

The strategy Roman learned at the hands of Don Sinchi mirrors the healing tradition that most Amazonian shamans have passed from generation to generation for centuries. It requires complete isolation from *everything*—including friends, family, distractions, even one's ordinary thought patterns—that might be a source of tension and might, deep within a person, be sponsoring their illness. This is what the next five weeks are going to look like—not only for our eight guests, but, to a different degree, for me and my crew as well.

● ● ●

At dusk the following day, my walkie-talkie bleeps to life with the raspy Spanish of Arbildo, the hired guardian of the institute. These lands are mostly safe, but there is the occasional dispute or local robbery, so Arbildo was brought on to keep a watchful eye over the perimeter of the nearly 1,000-acre plot of rain forest.

"The patients have arrived," he announces.

Everyone at the center hears him, and his words immediately set us in motion. By the time we have walked down the long, muddy path to the road, our new arrivals are standing outside the van they took from the plane, staring at the dark woods behind us in a combination of excitement and fear.

Gretchen, our patient with IBS, is the first to come forward. "Hi, Nick!" she says with a huge smile. "This is so cool. I can't believe we're actually here." We know from her application that Gretchen is a fearless lover of the outdoors who can hack it anywhere on the planet. For her, we think, the challenge will come in the ceremonial component.

"Is it always this rainy here?" asks Jessica. "I didn't bring any boots." She is clearly not as enthusiastic as Gretchen, having just endured a 24-hour journey from her home in Oklahoma in the middle of a serious flare-up of her Crohn's disease. We know from our periodic check-ins leading up to the trip that the lesions in her intestine have been worsening over the past two months, leading to some occasional equivocation on her part about whether this was really a good idea. It took a lot of guts for her to get on that plane.

"So good to see you all," I say, cheerfully attempting to hide my own internal butterflies. "You've all had quite a few days of travel, and I'm sure you're tired and hungry. It's a long walk to where you will each be staying, so let's head to the meeting house where we have supper prepared for you."

Twenty minutes later, everyone is seated at a long table in the meeting house, which, like every other structure in the jungle, is built from hand-hewn wooden planks, pruned and sanded tree branches, and a thatched roof of dried grass.

The light of day has now faded entirely, and the rain has started up again. The unrelenting barrage of water hitting the roof, leaves, and ground right outside the longhouse has a few of our new arrivals looking over their shoulder while trying to keep a positive expression. The thin screen walls do an okay job of keeping the bugs out, but the sounds of the jungle are right next to us at all times.

Juanita, our resident cook, brings out a giant pot of jungle vegetable and quinoa stew that is then portioned into eight bowls and placed before each patient.

As they begin to eat by flickering candlelight, Roman walks in from a side door and greets each guest one by one, welcoming them to the healing center with a warm smile. A sense of relief comes over the faces of our more burdened patients when they see the shaman. He is the reason they are here, and hopefully this man and the other two medicine men are the answer they have been seeking.

"We are honored that you have put your faith in us," he says. "Please relax and enjoy the food while I do my best to explain to you what we do here and what the next 30 days will look like." A kind of communal peace sets over the group as they eat.

"I am going to go straight to the point," Roman says after a while. "In order to heal oneself in Amazonian tradition, the individual must first learn how to make peace with all different aspects of their being. You now sit in the largest forest on planet Earth, and here, nature is seen as the divine teacher and healer.

"Sickness is not the enemy. It's a natural cue to help us recognize where we can learn more about ourselves and develop and evolve in our lives. When a patient comes to a shaman in the jungle, that healer doesn't fight the sickness or disease but instead follows along with it to help determine what that condition is attempting to communicate. Everything in the jungle is seen as an expression of divine intelligence.

"There is no good or bad; there is just information.

"Why do we insist on full immersion in nature within your own secluded *dieta* hut? Because this will help you slow down and begin to have a dialogue with yourself again. Through day after day of quiet contemplation, watching the seamless flow of energy from one plant to another and the interrelationship of all creatures of all sizes in one harmonious system, we begin to make inner connections. The ego becomes humble. In the West, our ego is indulged and inflated until it becomes the center of the universe. It does things on its own accord, doesn't consider the entire organism, and distorts our reality.

"This first week will be quite an adjustment for you, but once you begin to acclimate, you will start to see nature as a mirror for yourself. And in that mirror you will find much-needed answers that provide the road map to your healing journey."

The guests listen intently to what the shaman is saying, but a few of them are clearly concerned and possibly second-guessing whether they're up for what's ahead. Joel, our patient with type 2 diabetes, glances over his shoulder a few times as some kind of insect screeches in the rainy dusk. Nicola, our patient with Parkinson's, is smiling but clearly fatigued, having defied all odds just to make her 22-hour voyage from Southington, Connecticut, to where she now sits.

These patients clearly need treatment and rest right away. But before they can do that, they need grounding, an understanding of where they are and what's about to happen to them.

Roman continues. "The tribes in this region consider this medicine path to be an extreme intervention, only to be used by the very sick. And indeed, because of the intensity that is experienced, those who are not seriously ill don't usually feel it's worth the trial and tribulation they must endure. So I honor the eight of you for stepping forward, knowing that this won't be easy."

He goes on to explain the specific dietary regimens that he and the other shamans have put together for each guest based on his or her condition. "The food in the Amazon is delicious," he says, "but you will have to wait until some other point in your life to experience it."

Each patient will be on a shamanic nutritional protocol known as a *dieta* that is intended for sustenance, connection to the plants, and healing.

John, our patient with prostate cancer, speaks up. "Excuse me, Roman?" he says. "I am a vegan and my body needs plenty of fruit in order to stay in balance. Will special exceptions be made for those of us with specific dietary needs?"

"Good question," says Roman, thanking John. "You will each be receiving different herbs and meal plans based on your unique condition. But this will be decided by the medicine men, based on what they know will give you the best chance at leaving here healed."

There is a pattern in the Amazonian medicine approach, he explains. Anything that is distracting or comforting is removed so that patients can fully experience the parts of themselves that they would normally pacify with comforts like food and external distractions.

"I know that Nick had many long calls with each of you, going over exactly what you were in store for during your stay here," he says. "But the reality is always a little different and possibly more intimidating than we imagined." He pauses to look around at the group, and his eyes reflect the compassion mixed with sharp intelligence and unyielding will that I've come to consider Roman's hallmark. "Give yourself the space to feel any fear or anxiety tonight. It's totally natural. This is a foreign place, thousands of miles away from what many of you would consider the modern world. It's okay to be a little scared." Though his words are meant to soothe, the subtext is clear: no deviations from the prescribed healing path will be permitted—without exception.

After another brief pause, Roman goes on to cover two housekeeping issues. First, he advises our guests to be ever vigilant in keeping their mosquito nets, or *mosquiteros*, tucked tightly around their beds at night. "The mosquitoes here are ruthless," he says. "And you won't feel them when they bite you. I have had patients wake up with hundreds of bites all over an arm that mistakenly flopped out of the net, without their having felt a thing. You don't want that to be you. Plus, there are poisonous spiders here that you would probably rather keep out of your bed."

Without pausing for comment, he gives them the other bad news. "As Nick already told you, we do not allow any man-made distractions here at Paititi. This means no mobile phones, no computers, iPod, radio, or any other electronic devices. It also means no books, no magazines, no crossword puzzles, games, or other ways to pass the time. I know that most of you at least brought a phone with you in order to find your way here, but you have no need for it now. Before you make your voyage out to your new homes, please make sure to leave any of these things here on the table, and we will keep them in a dry and secure place for the duration of your stay."

Item number one about the mosquitoes earns Roman some wide-eyed responses, but it isn't nearly as alarming as number two. I had a feeling this might happen, even though I made it clear to each patient before accepting their application that books and electronics were not allowed. This prompts questions from the patients about what qualifies as a man-made device—spiritual coloring books, drawing paper and colored pencils, books of prayer, diaries and journals.

It turns out that all of these, aside from a simple journal and pen, must be relinquished before the patients' departure into the deep woods. Some of the sicker ones don't blink an eye at this, but a few of our younger guests are noticeably perturbed. I can almost read their minds as they weigh their emotions against the inevitability of the situation they've signed up for. Arguing with your hosts is not the best idea when they are the only people you know in one of the most extreme environments on the planet.

"You have all made quite a journey today," Roman says at last. "I'm sure you must be tired. We will be visiting with each of you in the morning and can answer any of your other questions at that time. For now, let's finish our supper and get you each settled in your quarters."

The patients finish their soup in silence. The discomfort and urgency in some of these people is now beginning to reveal itself. In a few minutes, each of them will begin the small trek out to their one-room, thatch-roofed domiciles, many of which are tucked in remote plots of jungle. Some are so far into the forest that even a scream or yell wouldn't reach the ears of any other patient, shaman, or staff member.

This is going to be one of the toughest months that any of us have ever had.

THE PATH OF NO DISTRACTIONS

In Amazonian healing protocols, every aspect of your existence is taken into consideration. When you show up for a healing intervention in these circles, you are asked to surrender just about everything you own at the door.

This means cell phones, laptops, watches, jewelry, books of all types (yes, even the ones on shamanic healing, herbs, and spiritual coloring books). You are then led deep into the forest to your very own dieta hut—a screened-in, one-room structure with a thatched roof, a twin bed, a hammock, a small rough-hewn desk and chair, and that's it. This is where you will be spending your one-month to six-month stay.

Yes, you can wander outside your hut if you'd like, and occasionally go on solitary walks through the jungle, and maybe even jump into the river. But the majority of your waking hours are spent in this thinly screened-off enclosure, far from anyone—or anything—else.

Aside from the helpers and apprentices who bring you your meals and other jungle necessities like toilet paper and candles, the only visitors you can expect are the shamans. They come by one or two times a day to administer herbs, prayers, and hands-on healing—or to guide you through the forest to the sacred *maloka*, or jungle temple, where you sometimes spend the evening in ayahuasca ceremony. If you speak Spanish, you may find a willing ear for a bit of small talk, but most of the time the medicine men and women are all business.

The idea is to remove any outside stimuli that might distract you from doing the deep inner work that is required for the healing to take place. In the same way yogis use Vipassana meditation, sitting in utter silence for days to find lasting peace at a core level, the cultures of the Amazon use isolation in nature to dissolve the patient's ego and bring up any shadows that need to be confronted and purged.

This isn't always pretty.

We tend to indulge any externality that might give us quick comfort or excuse us from sitting in silence with ourselves and listening to what our hearts have to tell us. This can be as outwardly obvious as substance abuse or as subtle as workaholism on the part of someone who just doesn't have the time to slow down and smell the roses for a second.

Everyone has a pacifier—and when you take it away, things tend to get real.

Chapter 6

◇◇◇◇◇◇◇◇◇◇◇◇◇◇

MEDICINAL HERBS AND HOW THE SHAMANS FIND THEM

If the Amazon rain forest is an encyclopedia of medicinal plants, the indigenous cultures who dwell there are its index and table of contents.

—MARK PLOTKIN, ETHNOBOTANIST

In the Western world, herbs are ingested in much the same fashion that a pill might be. They're put into a capsule or pressed into a pill and swallowed with some water. This is not an altogether ineffective method, if the ingester is seeking solely to access the plant's physical constituents. But what is largely overlooked in the modern world is a medicinal plant's subtle energetics, or as it is known in many indigenous cultures, its spirit.

This is another one of those concepts that a stranger to these traditions might find delightfully imaginative and great fodder for an anthropology lesson about the incredible deities and magical rites that more primitive societies tend toward. This is exactly how I felt when I first was introduced to the concept of plant spirits. They were just fairy tale explanations of scientifically verifiable chemical effects of a given root, leaf, or flower—kind of like Native Americans calling the long rifle a "thunder stick" before they began to understand how gunpowder worked and started using it themselves.

Navigating the waters of magico-spiritual traditions is tricky that way. Sometimes you come across an extravagant explanation for a very simple principle established in modern science centuries ago. But woven into our ancestral tapestry are some extremely powerful and "lost" threads of understanding that simply do not fit into the reason-based Western notion that it doesn't exist if we can't measure and replicate it.

The concept of subtle plant energetics and plant spirits fall into this second category. If you don't believe me, just ask them. Yes, I mean the plants.

We've all heard that talking to your plants when you water them makes them happy. This is explained away by modern science as a simple gift of carbon dioxide from our spoken exhalations that plants happily absorb, but there might be more to it than that.

Herbalists have been communicating directly with plants for millennia. It's a very subtle art that requires an open heart and a clear and meditative mind focused fully on the matter at hand. But once we human beings begin to tap into our sixth sense— our intuition—phenomena like plant energetics become far easier to fathom.

In the Amazon, the dieta is the preferred method of connecting with a particular plant to learn all of the lessons it has to teach. An individual ingests a particular plant, usually with the advice of a shaman, for an extended period of time until the spirit of that plant makes itself known to him or her through dreams, intuitive communications, sensations in the body, and other immeasurable occurrences that only the individual and the plant are privy to. It's an entirely experiential practice that can be used with all edible and medicinal herbs, but it requires discipline and a very simple diet that doesn't interfere with the fragile character of the plant.

Our patients are all on a dieta of sorts. Joel and Juan are on the purest form of dieta, taking only one medicinal herb every day, other than the ayahuasca and San Pedro cactus they ingest during ceremonies. The others are taking a combination of complementary herbs that each treat a specific aspect of their illness. Our breast cancer patient, Melinda, for example, is being treated topically with aloe-based herb poultices while also drinking a tea of graviola and *uña de gato* before breakfast and dinner.

But even for those who are working with multiple plants, the shamans emphasize in their daily visits to each hut the importance of being still and connecting with the energies of the plants they are taking. Before each cup of tea is administered, a long prayer is sung over the liquid and offered with reverence from medicine man to patient.

These herbs are prescribed by both Edwin and Habin, but their methods for determining what a patient needs are extremely different.

On the fourth morning after the patients arrive, Edwin invites a couple of us to accompany him and his son, named Christian, on a walk deeper into the jungle to collect more medicine for the patients. Christian is slightly taller than his father and almost always smiling whenever I've seen him passing through the forest. He is apprenticing under Edwin to become a shaman himself.

We quickly grab one of our cameras, some sound gear, and a jug of water, and go.

This is a dream of a filmmaking scenario for us, tailing a medicine man and his apprentice on a whim as they plod into the jungle, over fallen trees that bridge fingers of river, under low-hanging vines and leaves the size of elephant ears, trying to keep up.

After about an hour of walking, the character of the landscape around us changes drastically. The trees are becoming much larger, some thicker than a school bus. The sounds of the animals are changing too. Large birds and some type of monkey can be heard in the canopy above us.

"Estamos entrando en la antigua selva," Edwin calls back to us as he hacks his way through the branches that are crisscrossing the overgrown footpath ahead. We are entering the old jungle.

Edwin walks gracefully through the undergrowth, machete in hand and small hatchet on his belt, with his apprentice following closely behind. What looks like a dense tangle of vines, leaves, and flowers is something entirely different to the vegetalista. He knows the medicine he's after, but along the way he calls out the names and uses of scores of herbs growing on and around the trees we pass.

He stops at a cluster of vines pouring down the side of a tree. "This one here is known as *itininga,*" he says. "The people here have made baskets from this material since ancient times." A few moments later, we're standing in front of a tree that to my untrained eye looks no different from the others surrounding it. "This tree is called *chuchuhuasi,*" says Edwin. "I use the bark to treat rheumatism and pain in the joints and back. Not many know about this one. Christian," he instructs his apprentice, "cut a few of the leaves off that branch, please." The young man harvests a few wide leaves and places them in his sack.

We climb a small ridge and drop into a gully carved by a stream we've been following. The temperature instantly drops by five degrees, and the sound of the jungle intensifies with the addition of a high-pitched insect howl. Edwin doesn't seem to notice the change as he stops by an unspectacular shrub. This one is similar to the others crowding around it, but with slightly darker leaves and spikes here and there along its stems. *"Mucura,"* pronounces Edwin. "The leaves of this one are used to heal cancer of the breast." Edwin nods to Christian, who is already approaching one of the trees with a machete to strip some of the bark.

Edwin's knowledge clearly comes from a long life of hands-on experience alongside other plant maestros, the same experience Christian is getting by quietly shadowing him—machete in one hand and a sharp ax in the other. Where we see a dense patch of foliage, Edwin sees a well-labeled, living medicine cabinet.

Of the three shamans we're working with, Edwin strikes me as the most scientific. He isn't sensing the right plants to harvest, but instead relying on decades of teaching from others before him.

We scramble up the other side of the large trench and make our way down the narrowing trail until it disappears completely. "A little farther this way," Edwin says. "We're almost there."

Almost where? I wonder. We're in the middle of nowhere and now without an obvious way back. The realization is slowly creeping in that our fate is in this shaman's hands now. It would be very difficult to find our way back without him.

"Christian, look. There it is." Edwin points with his machete up through the canopy at a towering tree that is at least 100 feet taller than the others around it.

That must be a lupuna. I've heard Roman and Habin talk about this tree, but according to their stories, it doesn't grow anywhere near civilization, at least not anymore. They are under serious threat from illegal logging and can usually only be found a few days' hike into the old-growth forest.

There's an old legend told among the local lumberjacks that these magical trees will exact revenge on anyone who harms them. Some refuse to go near them for fear that they will befall some terrible fate if they so much as urinate nearby.

"Come." Edwin beckons us to follow him in the direction of the beautiful giant. "It's farther away than it looks." He's right—it takes us the better part of 10 minutes to reach it.

The lupuna is larger than any other tree in the tropics and can be as wide as 33 feet and as tall as 250 feet when given the time to grow. It's considered by the local tribes to be the guardian of the jungle and extremely powerful.

Aside from its staggering size, the *Chorisia integrifolia* distinguishes itself from other tropical trees because of its belly, a part of the trunk that is wider than the rest and bears some resemblance to a human abdomen.

As we approach, Edwin begins to explain to us the reason we left the beaten path 30 minutes ago and ventured all this way into the bush. "In order to initiate a healer or shaman the way I was initiated, you must first drink ayahuasca 12 times. Christian, my eldest son here, has just completed his 12th ceremony, and his body has begun a deep purification process. Now he must prepare himself a very strict dieta of the sacred lupuna tree to complete this preliminary stage of his journey."

Edwin turns toward the tree, puts his hand on a patch of bark about three feet from the ground, and traces an invisible square on its surface. He then brings his ear close to the bark and listens for a few moments.

"Christian, hand me the ax." Christian slides the ax off his shoulder and into both hands, presenting it to his father.

Dan and I look at each other in confusion and slight alarm. *There's no way he going to start hacking at this sacred tree, is he?* Sensing our concern, Edwin explains. "We are going to take a patch of bark, from which we will extract sap for the ceremony. This is done in a special way so that the tree can repair itself. Trust me, we will not be hurting the lupuna—it wouldn't be a good idea."

With that, Edwin turns back toward the tree, once again traces out the invisible square, and chips carefully along the imaginary marks. Liquid begins to trickle from the fresh wound. Ten minutes later, he completes a square the size of a cereal box, exposing some of the white inner wood in his deep cuts. With some effort, he uses the flat of the ax to pry the square from the tree. Christian catches it in a piece of cloth as it falls.

Edwin turns to his son and pulls a small wooden cup from his pack. Christian puts down the lupuna slab and takes the cup from the shaman's hands. The square of tree flesh at our feet is oddly soft on the underside, and Edwin easily tears off a handful of pulp, which he then squeezes into the vessel.

Out of his pocket comes a *mapacho* cigarette, one of the local sacraments of this region, rolled from powerful jungle tobacco. He lights it up and begins to pray over the cup and its fluids in a mixture of Spanish and Quechua, giving thanks to the tree, to Pachamama, and asking for clear-sightedness and strength to be bestowed upon his son as he enters the realms of the sacred.

He nods to Christian, who brings the cup up to his lips and then closes his eyes as he drinks it down. His eyes open again and he stares into Edwin's eyes.

"*Ya. Listo.*" All right. Ready to go.

I'm not sure what I was expecting. The apprentice didn't turn into a jaguar or levitate off the ground after drinking from the sacred tree, the way it might have played out in a fantasy novel. But in that moment after drinking, something subtle seemed to transpire between shaman and apprentice that we were not privy to. As we trudge back in the direction of the center, I have a nagging sense of an understanding that is just outside my reach.

A few hours after we return, Roman and I are sitting in hammocks suspended from the eaves of the ceremonial *maloka* (temple) where he sleeps each night to be close to the patients. I give him the play-by-play of the lupuna ceremony, ending with the interaction that occurred in the few moments after the apprentice drank.

"It sounds like you witnessed a wordless conveyance of wisdom. Remember, this is a lineage of direct transmission. There has never been an interruption. For thousands of years, there was never a generation when there wasn't a living teacher to pass this knowledge to his students. This knowledge has been transferred in a state of being, not so much in the head but in the heart, in a state of openness, sincerity, and immersion in Mother Nature."

KNOW THE HERBS IN YOUR BACKYARD AND THEIR NATIVE USES

I'm driving down a dirt road in the high Kalamath Mountains, on my way to meet with a respected O'odham and Chicano elder, Dennis Martinez. I reached out to Dennis some months ago to ask if he would be willing to share some of his ancestral healing knowledge, but he's been in poor health lately, so the communication has been slow going. Finally, after a few months of back-and-forth, he gave me the green light to come.

The plan today is for us to go on a medicine walk so he can show me some of the native herbal remedies of the Northern California Highlands. It seems straightforward enough, but an all-too-familiar sense of nervousness sets in as I near his house.

Whenever I'm heading to meet with a tribal elder, I always get the jitters. I know in my heart that I was put here to do this work, and I've witnessed hundreds of universal signs supporting that truth. But working against me is that I'm a 6-foot-2 white guy with brown hair and blue eyes—a spitting image of your average settler from the 1700s.

Going into this work, you have to be aware of the damage that so-called wisdom seekers have done to these cultures. Many explorers have made contact, won the trust of medicine men and women, and studied under them, only to return to the modern world and use that tightly guarded knowledge to make a name for themselves—perhaps taking a potent and "undiscovered" herb to a pharmaceutical company, mass-marketing a new psycho-spiritual intervention, or (drumroll, please) writing a book that shares sacred and highly secretive practices—while positioning themselves as intrepid adventurers who risked life and limb to bring these pearls back to the masses.

Some native groups are still susceptible to this kind of exploitation, but the indigenous people of North America are anything but. Their past 400 years have been one long tale of trickery and betrayal at the hands of the white man, and they're very wise to the ego-driven agendas that many of us harbor.

Dennis and I squat by an old oak tree as he shows my team and me a particular area of tree bark that was harvested to treat respiratory issues. I've never heard of this remedy and suddenly feel obligated to warn him, "Dennis, are you sure you want this knowledge to be shared with everyone out there?"

His eyes peer through and beyond my pupils. I'm quite sure he's seeing everything that is going on inside me.

"There are things that we will not share with people outside of our tribe, powerful medicines and universal secrets that we've held close for generations. Our knowledge was once an open book, but we saw only immaturity and greed-driven mishandling of these herbs and rites in response. But this is not one of them. Trust me, if this oak medicine weren't to be shared, you and I would not be talking right now."

I've heard these words spoken by several First Nation elders, especially when they begin to get a better read on me. Before they will even meet, they ask about my intentions and who referred me, and they usually want a trusted mutual contact who can vouch for my integrity.

There exist schools of knowledge that will never be written about in a book or documented in a movie, because it simply isn't allowed anymore.

No matter where you live, I guarantee that yours is not the first human foot that stepped on that soil. We *Homo sapiens* have been here for a long time, and chances are very good that the flora and fauna in your neck of the woods have been studied intimately, tested, tuned in to, and used for a variety of physical, spiritual, and psychological purposes.

The notion that we need to venture off into unknown regions of the world to find our true nature is disrespectful to the very lands we were raised on. Plants were around a long time before we came into existence, and they've had a major hand in shaping who we've become.

If we want to attain a deeper understanding of the medicines that exist around us, we need to approach the learning process with humility. Start with some good research—you can learn many of the basics from a botanical guide about your local flora. Look for medicinal herb walks and workshops on how to wild-craft your own medicine, a practice going through a renaissance of popularity in the modern world.

If you want to go even deeper and reach out to indigenous wisdom keepers, make sure to do so with patience, permission, and respect.

Chapter 7

◇◇◇◇◇◇◇◇◇◇◇◇◇

THE JUNGLE
HEALING DIET

*Leave your drugs in the chemist's pot if
you can heal the patient with food.*

—HIPPOCRATES

**May 2, 2016
Tulum, Mexico**

I'm seated at a long dinner table on a stone patio of a Spanish
villa overlooking the Gulf of Mexico. To my left and right are a
number of prominent figures in the world of natural medicine
and nutrition. We've all been invited to this beautiful Mexican
home outside the ancient Mayan city of Tecal to meet minds and
find new ways of broadening the reach of this vital information.

Michelle and I sit side by side, listening to our three-year-old
son, River, play underneath a palm tree as a lavish dinner is laid
out before us all. With so many leaders in the natural-healing
world at the same table, you can imagine the variety of particular
dietary needs our tireless cooks have taken into consideration in
preparing this meal.

As we're eating, I notice a small bag of plantain chips tucked inconspicuously next to a steaming dish of gluten-free organic root vegetable soup (with a bone-broth base). I'm assuming a local must have forgotten these here after setting the table. Instinctively, I grab the bag and show it to Michelle, who responds with a big grin. We tear open the bag and begin to sneak chips into our mouths.

I feel a nudge on my elbow from my neighbor to the left—a very sweet and talented man named Rick whom I met the night before.

"Do you guys have a death wish? If half of these folks saw you eating those, they'd turn on you like a pack of wolves!" Rick's eyes are alight with amusement as he chides us under his breath.

Michelle laughs guiltily as I lean over to Rick. "I know, but it's totally worth the risk," I whisper confidentially. "Let me tell you a little story about how the fried plantain chip saved our asses in the jungle."

■ ■ ■

October 23, 2010
Loreto Province, Peru

It's day nine of our healing retreat, and the first week has been a big adjustment for the patients, who are each experiencing highs and lows. One morning the jungle feels like a paradise, and the next it feels like the worst mistake of your life. There is nothing to do during your waking hours but sit and observe the emotions that are passing through your body.

Snakes appear to be the forest friend to reckon with around these parts—as both patients and film crew are quickly learning. Sure, the black tarantulas are huge and, well, *around*, but they're fragile and relatively harmless. The snakes, on the other hand, can kill you quickly.

Last night Dan was walking back from Hut 5 by the light of a fading headlamp when he stopped to change the battery. As he was opening his pack, a 10-foot shushupe pit viper slithered between his feet on the narrow jungle path and out of sight on the other side. The shushupe (known as "the slow bringer of death") is legendary in these parts for its deadly venom but is rarely sighted because it's nocturnal.

Unfortunately, crazy people like us are too.

Today we're going to get our first hard reading of how the patients are doing. Dr. Oswald Pretel, a respected physician in the city of Iquitos, agreed to join our jungle staff for the retreat and will be performing his first round of checkups on the patients to see how their bodies are responding to the treatment, diet, and overall experience. Many here are hoping that the hardships of their initial adjustment period will be offset by some good news.

We split the film team into two units for the day, one to follow Dr. Pretel and me as we visit the patients and another to continue filming the regular activities around the camp. There were a few slipups on our end in the first few days and one or two incredible movie moments were missed, so we've made a pact to always have two separate teams filming in separate locations throughout the day. When we finally get back to the States and the editing room, this documentary will probably be cut down to 90 minutes or less—but at the pace we're going, there will be more than 250 hours of footage shot by Day 31.

Alberto, Dan, and I head out to meet Dr. Pretel at the main lodge, where we find him and Roman sitting at the dining table, discussing one of the patient files. We exchange greetings and get right to business.

"Nick, as you know, we have been monitoring basic vital signs each day and doing weekly blood work, but today we're going to try to get an assessment of the progress that each patient is making."

In addition to Dr. Pretel, a nurse named Kelly has also been seeing the patients every other day since their arrival, reporting directly back to him. Their white shirts, neatly groomed hair, and overall hygiene are in stark contrast to our own rugged exteriors.

The first hut we visit is Joel's. Joel, our type 2 diabetes patient from Tampa Bay, Florida, has been having a particularly hard time adjusting to jungle life. Through a couple of strained conversations with him in the past week, he's made it clear to us that he thought the facility was going to be more modern and closer to civilization. He really doesn't like spiders and had an uncomfortable run-in with a tarantula a few nights ago.

We make our way down the narrow dirt path to his hut, and he is already standing outside with a toothy smile, waiting to greet us. I guess he doesn't have much else going on today.

"Hi, Joel. How are you feeling this morning?" Roman asks.

"I'm doing great." Joel welcomes us into his little room as he responds. "I brought my own equipment to test my blood, and this morning I took a reading and I was shocked. My blood sugar is at 60 right now. It's never been that low. That's what my kids' blood sugar is at—you know, I've got young kids who like to test their blood when I do mine, so I know what their number is, too. My blood sugar has dropped from 190 when I got here to 60 as of this morning. That's lower than my kids'," he repeats, beaming at us while talking a mile a minute.

Roman translates everything into Spanish for Dr. Pretel, who doesn't speak English fluently, and the physician's brows go up as he hears the blood count.

"May I?" Pretel asks as he points to Joel's portable blood glucose meter. It's a nice one. "We took some blood samples from you on your second day here, correct?"

Roman translates and Joel nods while the doctor looks through his file and locates the numbers from that test. "Ah, interesting. You were at 190 when you first arrived, and that was taken before you ate breakfast. Have you eaten yet today?"

"No, my breakfast usually comes in about an hour. Usually right about when the sun reaches that branch up there." Joel lowers his tone and adds, "They don't let us keep clocks or anything electronic here." Pretel's modern appearance must give the impression that he's not in on all the happenings here, or that he'll be sympathetic to the deprivations Joel has endured.

"So you have been eating the regular diet and just taking the jungle herbs that are being prescribed to you. You're off all of your medications?"

"Yes, sir. They took all my medications at the door. I'm just doing what they tell me."

Pretel looks at Roman to confirm. Roman nods.

"Well, this is very good news. Keep doing what you're doing and we'll check back in a few days."

Joel excitedly shakes hands with the doctor and Roman as we leave.

Well, that's certainly a good start to the day. Dr. Pretel asks Roman exactly what herbs Joel has been taking. "A plant called *papailla* and the bark of the *tahuari* tree. You can speak with Edwin if there are any other questions."

We walk farther down the trail and split off on a narrow side trail toward Jessica's dieta hut. At first it doesn't look like anyone is inside, but my eyes adjust to the dark interior and make out a lump in a hammock strung across from the bed.

"Hello." Jessica's voice and demeanor are burdened, weak, but carry a hint of self-deprecating humor.

She has been suffering from Crohn's disease for years, and it has only become worse as of late. The agonizing patches of intestinal inflammation that are characteristic of the disease have advanced all the way down her digestive tract into her colon. There is very little she can eat besides chicken broth and overcooked quinoa. The long trip here did not help matters at all.

A moment later, three of us are standing next to the woman who is clearly trying to keep her body still as she lays suspended within the woven fabric.

"How are you feeling, Jessica?" Dr. Pretel asks. "Roman tells me you haven't been eating much this past week."

"Yeah, that's normal for me. I know it doesn't seem like I'm eating much, but there actually has been some mild improvement in my pain since I got here. I haven't thrown up in a few days, which I take as a good sign."

"I see here that you are taking *sangre de grado, uña de gato,* and *guayusa* in the morning and evening. Roman, am I missing any?"

"Jessica is also participating in ayahuasca ceremonies, which have a strong effect on the digestive system, as you know. She is on a healing protocol very similar to what I was prescribed for my own Crohn's disease many years ago."

A momentary look of surprise flashes across Dr. Pretel's face before he remembers that Roman himself was acutely ill with the same disease 10 years ago.

"Well, we need to keep a close eye on this one," says Dr. Pretel. "Her tests show that she's anemic, and we need to make sure she gets more iron and overall calories into her system. I'm happy that the pain is improving, Jessica, but there is still a long way to go."

"I'll be back to work with you in a few hours, okay?" Roman has been administering some additional treatment to Jessica using a few energy healing protocols that helped him with his own recovery.

Jessica nods, and tears come to her eyes as we say goodbye.

We stop by Nicola's hut next. Our Parkinson's patient from Connecticut is reclining in her bed under her mosquitero as we enter. A beam of hot sun is spilling across her bundled midsection. Given the humidity and temperature this morning, I'm not sure how she's able to tolerate the heat. The only part of her that is uncovered is her face, and there are no signs of perspiration.

Her speech is heavily impaired by her condition, but she tells us she has been in bed resting after one of the best nights of sleep she has had in recent memory. Nicola then conveys a remarkable healing that she experienced yesterday during a personal session with Roman. She says something was released in her that has been locked away since "the accident."

The year before Nicola's Parkinson's symptoms came on, she was in a serious car accident that left her badly injured. In addition to broken bones, she endured severe whiplash that twisted one of her vertebrae out of position, leaving her with a permanent neck injury that prevented her from turning her head to the left or right.

When we visited her for her intake interview, we witnessed this limitation firsthand. In addition to the tremors and tightness associated with her Parkinson's, Nicola had no mobility in her neck. There was no casual turn of her face toward or away from the camera; this simple movement took great effort, requiring that she turn her entire body to make the adjustment.

"Watch this," she says, as a faint smile creeps across the increasingly responsive muscles of her face.

Her head slowly begins to swivel as she turns it all the way to the left to look over her shoulder at the forest outside. Such a simple yet monumental movement. She slowly turns it back to see us smiling broadly.

"I haven't been able to do that in five years. Just that. Imagine!" Nicola's voice seems to be a bit steadier now than it has been, and I detect the subtle elegance of an English accent where there hadn't been one just a day ago. There is someone being freed inside this woman whom the world hasn't seen for a long time.

"This is very impressive," Dr. Pretel says. "So in addition to the herbs you are taking, Roman has been doing some work on you. What kind of work?" The doctor has been brought into the fold on all of the treatments, meal plans, and ceremonies, but this "work" that Nicola received is news to him.

Roman speaks up before Nicola can answer. "Doctor, Nicola was feeling some pain and tension last night, so I performed a technique called cupping on her neck and upper spine to relieve it. I was taught this practice from a traditional Chinese medicine specialist some years ago and use it routinely now with locals who complain of similar issues."

The film team and I are already in on the scoop—we filmed the whole thing as it happened last night. The shaman first rubbed castor oil on his patient's neck and back and then took out two clear cups. Each of these tulip-shaped vessels has a small hole in the bottom through which air is sucked out using a little pump. This creates a vacuum that literally pulls skin and muscle away from the body. After positioning one cup directly on the back of her neck, Roman traced his fingers along the muscle until his index finger stopped on a point about three inches below and slightly to the left. He put the second cup on that point and began pumping the air out of both.

If you've never seen cupping in action, it's a pretty odd thing to behold. The cups come in various sizes for use in different applications. Depending on how much air is pumped out, the clear glass becomes filled with skin, giving the impression of a swelling boil or a bubble of flesh.

After the cups were emptied of sufficient air and filled about halfway with Nicola's skin and muscle tissue, Roman sang a short prayer in mixed Spanish and Quechua and then began gently moving them back and forth along some invisible axis or ridge that he alone could see.

About three minutes into the treatment, Roman said, "Nicola, do you feel that? I think I feel your vertebrae moving." A few seconds later we all heard a quiet pop as Nicola let out a long sigh. "There it is," said Roman, deep in concentration. "Keep breathing, Nicola. Is everything feeling okay?"

"I think so," she replied weakly. "There was a quick shot of pain, but it feels wonderful now. What did you do?"

"All I did with the cups is soften up the tight muscle and tissue around your neck bones and pull them out of the way. Your spine did the rest. Our bodies know which way they want to be aligned. We sometimes just need to get rid of the blockages."

Roman relays all of this to Dr. Pretel as the physician checks Nicola's pulse, lungs, and pupils. "And what are the herbs she is taking?" the doctor asks.

"We are giving her small doses of a plant called *chiric sanango*, which is also called 'a thousand needles.' The plant stimulates all the nerve endings in the body and is often used here for neurological disorders like Parkinson's. We are also considering a few *toé* ceremonies, once Habin gets here in a few days. But as you probably know, toé—*Brugmansia grandiflora*—is extremely dangerous and must be taken with extreme caution. I will let you know if we choose to go that route."

"Very good. I see both of these noted on the file here. Please keep me updated as to how the chiric sanango treatments go."

We leave Nicola and begin making our way out to huts four through eight, which are located deeper in the rain forest.

"Things are coming along very nicely with Nicola," observes Dr. Pretel as we walk. "I trust you will tell me before you add any additional treatments to a patient's healing plan?"

"Of course, maestro," the shaman responds, glancing back at me.

■ ■ ■

A few hours later, as we approach the last dieta hut, the tally is five to two. Five of our patients are experiencing very encouraging signs of improvement, and two are struggling but still optimistic. Our last visit, Roman tells the doctor, is to Garry, who has late-stage neuroendocrine cancer.

"How far away is he staying?" Dr. Pretel asks. "Not too far, I hope, with an illness like that."

"Another half mile, more or less."

Dr. Pretel looks at the shaman and then at me with an expression of concern that seems to be his resting face.

Upon arriving at the center, Garry politely insisted on taking Hut 8, the structure farthest away from the rest of the camp. His condition is advanced, and we've known his limitations since visiting him in his small apartment in Garibaldi, Oregon, a little over a month ago. But he's been a rugged outdoorsman his whole life and is one of the few patients who are comfortable being such a long distance from the center's main buildings.

The shamans and patient-care staff have been checking on Garry more frequently than they do the others, given his advanced state, and the 62-year-old deep-sea diver seems to have taken quite a liking to his outpost. From our longhouse to Hut 8 is about a 25-minute walk.

After about 10 minutes and a few stream crossings, we approach Garry's jungle residence, perched on the top of a little slope, looking down at the wetlands that we are currently trudging through.

He hears the crunch of our footfalls on the underbrush and shouts down to us, "Hey, fellas. Come on in!"

The screen door creaks as we pull it open, and we find him swinging in his hammock with his journal resting on his belly. There's a wide grin across his gray-bearded face.

"Good afternoon, Garry. How did you sleep?" Roman asks as the rest of us find some standing room.

Garry is exuberant. "I have trouble getting past the joy of this place at night," he says. "It's all romance. There's no fear involved in any of the sounds and creatures that come crawling around my hut. They're like, 'Hey, I'm over here! Somebody come and talk to me. No, I'm over here—' It's just beautiful, and not so loud that it's uncomfortable, but loud enough that it keeps your attention. I'm thrilled by it."

Dr. Pretel steps forward and gently puts his hand on Garry's forehead, which is glistening with a light sweat. "How are you feeling right now?"

"Well, I'm hesitantly optimistic. The intense pain in my stomach that's caused by the small tumors in my intestines is almost completely gone. This is a big deal. Since I was diagnosed, there have been days that I could barely move because the pain was so bad. These past few days, it's become more of a background noise that is much more tolerable. I'm not sure whether it's the herbs or the ceremonies, or both, but something is shifting for sure."

Even as he says this, we can hear labored breaths between his words. His demeanor is cheerful, but it's obvious the man is having some difficulty adjusting to the heat and the thickness of the air.

"That is great to hear," says Dr. Pretel. "Would you mind if I examine you?"

"Absolutely. Please do."

Garry raps with us about some of his adventures diving off the coast of his hometown in western Oregon with his core group of deep-sea buddies as the physician checks his vitals and listens to his chest cavity with his stethoscope.

"You are brave to make the long journey here from the United States, sir." Pretel's usually serious expression melts into kind-eyed admiration for the man lying in front of him. "The medicines of the jungle are powerful. A few of my own family members have recovered from their illnesses in exactly the same way you are attempting to. Good luck until my next visit, and please stay hydrated."

The sun is about halfway between high noon and dusk as we begin our long walk back to the meeting house. Once Garry is out of earshot, Roman turns to the physician, who appears deep in thought, and asks, "So, what do you make of it all?"

"I'm very happy with much of what we saw today. The patients seem to be thriving for the most part. But—" He stops for a brief moment and turns to look at Roman intently. "You must transfer Garry to a closer hut. It's very good that his pain has subsided, but the man is still in his final days with cancer. This is the responsible thing to do."

Roman puts up a few minutes of polite resistance, pointing out that it was Garry's choice to be on the outer limits alone, but he ultimately defers to the physician's judgment. "We will move him to Hut 6, one of our closest patient houses, tomorrow. I think Joel will be okay with switching."

With that settled, Dr. Pretel and the shaman begin to compare notes on each of the patients, coming to many of the same conclusions about how best to proceed. We carefully navigate the forest underbrush as the two healers from opposite backgrounds create a game plan for the next week.

They begin to speak in greater depth and their cadence becomes quicker. After a few minutes, I get tangled in some of the Spanish medical terminology and check out of the conversation, letting the jungle noises and sensations wash over me for a minute.

We walk by a trail that leads off down a small slope to the bank of a babbling stream, ending at the hut belonging to our prostate cancer patient, John. I can just barely make out the thatched roof of his residence in the distance, and I wonder how he's doing. Of all our patients, John is the one who has struggled most with the deeper aspects of himself. As he describes it, he has always chosen to be a lone wolf, not part of the pack. Somehow in the jungle, despite his isolation, he is feeling this choice more deeply than he ever has before, and at the same time he's struggling with the concept of relinquishing control of his health care, his daily routine, and especially his diet to others, even those he believes hold his best chance of beating cancer.

His exasperated outbursts of rage have been cast at everyone from the staff who brings his food to Roman himself (the latter much more frequent and intense), but we all recognize that John is merely fighting the same battle all our patients are facing in one manner or another, though perhaps externalizing a bit more.

Our guests are in solitary confinement out here, with doors that open onto dense jungle that is teeming with fauna and flora. There is no running water or electricity. The only other amenity they have is the little wooden outhouse that accompanies each building, which is nothing more than a shack on top of a deep hole in the ground—plus whatever critters might have decided to take up residence.

There is no escape—from your environment, from your thoughts, or from yourself.

But something is happening out here that we as filmmakers are on the outside of. While we are busily shooting a documentary on each patient's experience and helping run the retreat itself, there is an inner adjustment or immersion gradually taking hold of them each day between our visits.

After a few days of initial turmoil as they settled in, everything seems to have quieted down. Each of our guests has begun to surrender to the environment they're in, almost as if the spirit of Pachamama is beginning to take hold of them, whispering secrets that only they can hear.

It's inspiring, but also somewhat eerie to witness.

■　■　■

The film crew and I don't have it quite as tough as the patients do. When we're not rolling camera, we stay in a longhouse constructed in much the same way as the dieta huts, but spacious enough to sleep 10 people comfortably. Total isolation isn't a part of our daily reality.

Still, we're working extremely long days in the heat, with no access to any comforts from the outside world. Our cameras are the only semblance of modernity we possess, but wielding these heavy beasts often feels like more of a burden than not having them at all. We're filming patients as they go through their personal and occasionally hellish trials in an effort to overcome their illnesses. It's an intense and trying environment that can disorient you if you're not focused.

We're eating the same limited diet as the patients, working in the same oppressive heat, and sitting in many of the same healing ceremonies that they are. Each day the hum of the rain forest is penetrating deeper, revealing more about each of us. With no electricity, hot water, or other basic amenities of home, the only choice is to embrace the way of the locals.

I handpicked this team not only for their film experience but also for their ability to handle themselves calmly in intense situations. These are extraordinary individuals, but even the strongest is challenged in an environment like this.

■ ■ ■

The loud hum of our winged and scaled forest friends is beginning to subside as the sun comes up on Day 12. I'm mostly awake, plodding through blue-green forest toward the community well where we all get our water and take care of basic morning and evening hygienic needs. The generator-powered well pump is rumbling when I get there, and I see Alberto brushing his teeth over a small bucket resting on a nearby ledge.

"You're up early," I say. "Couldn't sleep?" It's not unusual to see someone down here at this hour, but Alberto is definitely not an early riser.

"I'm catching a ride to Cahuide. I hear there's a little restaurant there that makes eggs and yucca fries. Want to come? It's only a mile or two from here."

I squeeze paste onto my toothbrush and run the bristles across my molars for a few seconds to buy myself time to formulate a diplomatic response. Alberto is an impressive sound technician and indispensable in the field, but I've learned the hard way that he's extremely sensitive to criticism.

"Alberto, I need you here. And we all agreed that we're in this with the patients and won't cheat on the meal plan. If the staff finds out that we're sneaking around, it'll cause a rift. We need to be a team right now."

"I'm not having fucking quinoa and manzanita tea for breakfast again today," Alberto says in exasperation. "You want us to be filming twelve hours a day in the middle of the heat and rain, getting bitten by god-knows-what, and I'm fine with that. All I'm asking for is some eggs."

The leaves on the path behind us crunch as Dan makes his way down the path in our direction. "What's going on?"

"I'm heading to Cahuide for breakfast if boss will let me. Want to come?"

"Wait, I thought we had a pact that the jungle diet applies to all of us." Dan looks at me and I can see his play. He overheard our conversation and is down here playing dumb to help me reel in Alberto.

"Listen," I say. "I'm not loving the food here either. If I hadn't made a commitment to this process, I'd wander down the road at lunchtime and see if anyone had a beer and some fried fish, but it's not what we agreed to. Every one of you signed on to this film knowing what it was going to take. I'm asking you to keep your word to me and the rest of the team." Dan nods in agreement.

Outnumbered, Alberto mutters something under his breath about this not being optimal to his unique dietary needs and takes his leave of us, trudging off deeper into the jungle in the direction away from the road and Cahuide.

"He just needs to walk it off. This place gets to you, know what I mean?" Dan speaks while we both watch him disappear into the bush.

"As long as he's back when we start filming in an hour, he can do whatever he needs to do."

We both know he'll be back. Where else is there to go?

Connected to the mission, but alarmingly disconnected from the outside world we once knew, we must navigate every day with care. Each of us is beginning to realize that we have no more reprieve from this jungle healing experiment than the patients do. And the truth isn't always pretty.

THE HEALING DIET

The jungle diet is very basic, intended for sustenance, not pleasure. After all, pleasure is at its core simply a means of distraction. The jungle diet consists of boiled and roasted green plantains, well-cooked root vegetables like yucca and cassava, a bony and flavorless local fish called *bocachico*, quinoa, very simple broths, and sometimes jungle fruit like papaya and coconut for breakfast. There is little to no salt, no spices, and absolutely no animal fats on this meal plan.

The shamans believe that the delicate life energies and compounds in each of the herbs that are being prescribed, including the *Banisteriopsis caapi* vine (one of the ingredients in ayahuasca), can be easily diluted and destroyed if the patient eats too heavy a diet. Contrary to the detox diets that are popular in the modern world, which consist of green smoothies, lemon cayenne shots, and saltwater liver flushes, the foods that are prescribed here are bland and relatively devoid of any palate-satisfying sensation.

Even a raw vegan diet can thrill the taste buds, but not this one. No comfort or escape to be found in the cuisine that is coming out of the Paititi kitchen hut.

The principles of this food regimen stem from the traditional dieta used by shamans, apprentices, and patients in this region of the world. In order to understand and harness a healing plant's power, the patient needs to keep a very pure diet that doesn't interfere with the subtle energetics and overall character of the medicinal herb.

In addition to the sustenance-only food options, the patient is strongly advised to abstain from sex or any stimulation in that region whatsoever during the healing dieta—in this case 32 days—for similar reasons. The medicine men and women strongly believe that every bit of the patient's focus and life force needs to be preserved and concentrated on the healing task at hand.

It makes you think. We run around this world chasing after every sparkly object, pouring our precious, finite energy into anything we chance upon. This work is not about finding some miracle cure that exists outside us, but about getting rid of the blocks and leaks that are inhibiting our ability to see clearly and heal ourselves.

This powerful ancient dieta practice can be done anywhere on the planet—and has been for thousands of years. The language and rituals around it are the only things that vary.

Alberto returns 30 minutes later, apologizes gruffly for his momentary lapse of team spiritedness, and starts putting his audio gear together for the day's filming assignments. It's what I expected he'd do, but there's an inner sigh of relief just the same.

I've gotta figure out some way of giving these guys a break.

Later that day, as the sun is setting, the crew and I are busy logging the footage from the day when we hear footsteps approaching. It's the guard Arbildo, walking and whistling toward our longhouse with a bulging plastic sack hanging from one of his hands. It's a Herculean bag of fried plantain chips.

When we see this golden treasure, every activity in our quarters comes to a crashing halt.

"I was in Iquitos today and bought some plátanos for you all at Belén market. These are the best I've ever had. Want a treat?"

Arbildo has long since left the tribal ways and isn't familiar with the rigid dietary protocol we're adhering to. He's more than happy to share his heavenly fried plantain chips with our haggard group of gringo filmmakers.

"Please, for the love of god, can we eat this man's chips?" Alberto pleads. "They fell right into our lap." His entreaty starts off serious, but the corner of his mouth curls as he tries to hold back a smile.

I look at Brock, Dan, and Michelle, who are staring at the plastic sleeve of greasy gold. The decision has already been made.

"Nobody hears about this, agreed?"

That night, we sit huddled around the miraculous sack of chips and savor every crispy bite, unbeknown to the shamans and patients. Like children who are getting away with the most punishable of crimes, we grin at one another by candlelight.

The salty oil on our fingertips is a dose of home that soothes something deep inside us, but it's also a sobering reminder of how far we are from the lives we know.

■ ■ ■

May 2, 2016
Tulum, Mexico

The Yucatan breeze picks up as Michelle and I finish telling Rick and his partner our story of plantain chips in the Amazon. Paleo-friendly, low-glycemic cuisine is being served on the Mexican terrace where we sit, and other guests are beginning to take notice of our intimate huddle at the end of the long table. Somewhere during the story, we instinctually slid our chairs closer together like coconspirators in a secret plot.

"Tell me what happened next. Which patients were cured? We need to know!" Mission accomplished. Rick is clearly no longer concerned about the negative health impact of our plantain chips.

"That's all I can tell you. You'll have to watch the movie to find out."

As the health food comes our way, Michelle and I quickly devour every remaining plantain chip in the mysteriously placed little bag. We offer the last one to Rick, who accepts it like a wafer at Sunday mass.

"Delicious."

GRANDPA'S KITCHEN: MASTERING THE BASICS WITH REVERENCE

My uncle John tells a great story about his first encounter with his stepfather, my late grandfather on my father's side, after whom I was named. He met my grandmother a few years after World War II, when he was in his early 30s, and it was love at first sight.

My grandmother, Frances Elrose, always told us he was the most handsome man she had ever seen—and oh, what a beautiful car he had! But she had a complicated life when they first encountered each other.

A year before they met, my grandma had done something that was unspeakable in those days. After ten years in an unhappy marriage, she had made an unconventional choice and decided to amicably separate from her husband. This left her fending for herself and her two sons, John and Joe, with only the meager livelihood from her job as a beautician.

My uncle John was only seven when he was first brought to meet his mom's hot new romance. Like most kids in this situation, he wasn't too excited about this man who was trying to take the place of his father. John was determined not to befriend this intruder.

They walked into the kitchen of my grandpa's Brooklyn apartment and there he was, with his back to them, pulling things out of the refrigerator, getting ready to cook.

He turned and saw them in the doorway. "You must be John. Say, can I make you some scrambled eggs for breakfast?"

"Eggs? I don't like eggs," my young uncle said defiantly.

Smiling, my grandpa leaned across the counter. "Oh, I promise you'll like mine."

With that, he cracked two eggs in a pan coated with butter and did what we've all seen him do hundreds of times since. He created the most delicious eggs of all time.

My grandpa won his future stepson over that morning. From that day forward, he and my uncle began to trust and ultimately develop a deep love for each other.

Watching my grandpa cook was one of the most therapeutic experiences of my childhood. The man did everything with such care and intention, from slicing an onion to sprinkling a little extra dried basil on top of a marinara sauce to hand-drying the pan after the meal was over. Each step was performed with reverence, carefully following some inherited code of culinary ethics.

There was nothing too simple or basic for his skilled hands. Anything that came into his awareness was treated as though it were the only thing in the universe at that moment.

The first thing he ever taught me to cook was an egg. In his opinion, mastering the perfect egg was one of the hardest things to do in the kitchen. If you understood the subtle effects of hot stainless steel and butter on a yolk and white, you could apply these to almost any other dish, simple or complex.

First there is the heat at which you cook your egg. Some might be tempted to crank it up to high, because technically, eggs are fried. But there is a sweet spot that isn't uniform across all stovetops. It has to be sensed with the hand held about five inches above the flame or electric burner. Somewhere between medium and high is the point at which a pat of butter will melt and sizzle but will not smoke. This is the right heat for egg making.

There's nothing else in the natural world that behaves quite like an egg when it's cracked open into a hot pan. The character changes from liquid goo into something beautifully symmetrical right before your eyes. Who was the first person to discover this culinary secret? Like most culinary leaps, it probably happened accidentally. An egg falls from a tree onto a hot rock that has been baking in the sun all day. A two-legged passerby takes notice while walking through the woods and calls his or her clan mates over. Somebody is brave enough to have a taste. Evolution.

If you think about it, the egg is essential to just about every culture of food worldwide, accepted by all. Baked goods, desserts, sauces, soups, deep-fry batters, mayonnaises and dressings, not to mention breakfast, would not be the same without this oblong cornerstone.

The second rule of perfectly cooked eggs is to know what to look for. The scrambled egg, when closely watched, gives all kinds of cues that let the cook know when it's time to push, pull, and flip with a spatula: how the bubbles are forming in the middle, how the edges ripple in spatters of grease, the thickness of the underbelly that is making contact with the pan. There is information in all of these visual indicators, and making perfect scrambled eggs requires attention to each one. Otherwise you'll wind up with something that is probably edible but is miles from taste bud bliss.

Last and possibly most important, a master knows how and when to touch the egg during its brief rendezvous with the frying pan. Because of its name, many make the mistake of literally scrambling their egg to death, swashbuckling with their spatula until all that remains is a mushy mess. This is not the way of the enlightened scrambler. Every touch changes the texture of your egg, and each move must be done with finesse. The fluffy, moist, and savory scramble that you might encounter at a high-end breakfast joint takes only four for five touches with a utensil to make.

Grandpa Nick taught me that the right pan with good heat and proper shortening will take care of 90 percent of the process. From there, it requires only an attentive eye and a steady hand to create the perfect egg.

My grandfather was this way about everything. Full presence. That's how he was taught by his dad. He never became too good at something to spend that extra time and dedication on the most basic task. Everything mattered. Everything was sacred.

The notion of quality tends to carry with it a connotation of the "old-fashioned" way. Back when things were done right, by hand, with care, nearby. When craftsmanship actually meant something. But the underlying principle of quality is much older than the words *old-fashioned* would lead us to believe. It boils down to an essential mantra that is downright ancient:

Master the basics and the rest will follow.

Chapter 8

◇◇◇◇◇◇◇◇◇◇◇◇◇◇

LIFE AND DEATH

October 26, 2010
Loreto Province, Peru

It's the 12th night since the healing retreat began, and the team and I are packing it in for the evening in our sleeping quarters on the second floor of the thatch-roofed longhouse. Dan and Alberto are lounging in hammocks discussing the highlights of the day, while Michelle logs some final notes about the developments with each patient on a large sheet of drawing paper spread across the wood-plank floor. Brock is at his usual evening post at a laptop in the corner, squeezing out the last of our fading battery power to back up all the footage from the day.

I'm fussing with a mosquito net when the walkie-talkie crackles on. "Nick and Roman, please come to Hut 6 right away." It's Andrea, one of our aides, who is on the early night shift, making rounds to ensure each patient has what he or she needs before bed. She is trying to keep an even tone as she speaks, but the urgency in her voice is clear.

Hut 6 is Garry.

"Copy that. Andrea, is everything okay?"

Silence. Then, "It's an emergency. Come right away."

I turn toward the team and Brock is already putting his boots on. "I'm coming with you."

Thirty seconds later, the two of us are running through dark jungle in the direction of Garry's hut—down a winding trail, across a stream on a small bridge, and up the opposite bank. Five minutes later, we see the shadow of the maloka looming against the night sky as we approach.

"Roman!" I yell up into the attic of the ceremonial temple where the shaman usually sleeps in order to be close to the patients at night, in case of scenarios like this. At Dr. Pretel's suggestion, we recently persuaded Garry to move to the dieta hut closest to the maloka.

No answer. He must already be there.

Branches whip at us as we barrel through the woods, just beginning to make out the faint flicker of headlamps and hushed voices through the trees.

A few seconds later, we see what all the lights are trained on. A pale, half-naked figure is slumped over on the wooden front steps of the hut, surrounded by four dark silhouettes.

"Garry, keep talking. Tell us what you are feeling right now." Roman has his hand on Garry's bare back. Edwin, Habin, and the nurse Kelly look up at us as we draw closer.

"I'm so hot," says Garry. "Hi, Nick." Garry's voice is labored but still has the warm and friendly note that has won the hearts of everyone now standing by his side. Edwin steps forward with a wet towel and wipes Garry's forehead and back.

"I'm having a hard time getting enough air."

"Take nice, easy breaths, my friend." Roman is pressing his fingers on a few points along Garry's arm.

"Hard to breathe—" The words fall short as his eyes squeeze shut, body suddenly slumping toward the ground. Two of us step forward and catch him as he tips off the steps.

"Garry. Garry?" Roman slaps him hard across the face. "Garry!" His face is blank, his large frame motionless.

"He's not breathing. I am going to start CPR," Roman says.

The six of us crouch beside Garry as Roman props up his chin, opens his airway, and stacks two hands on his bare chest. With elbows locked, he pumps downward while counting under his breath, "One, two, three . . ." Administering cardiopulmonary resuscitation in textbook fashion, Roman glances up at me with an expression I will never forget. This is the first and only time I have ever seen a look of fear on the shaman's face.

After 30 compressions, Roman opens Garry's mouth, makes sure the airway is clear, pinches his nose, and blows a full breath into his lungs. His sternum rises faintly as the air expands his chest. After delivering a second breath, Roman brings his ear up to Garry's nose and mouth, listening for any sign of respiration.

"Come on, Garry. Stay with us." The color is steadily draining from Garry's face, as a light drizzle begins to fall on us all. While Roman works, Kelly puts her index and middle fingers on his neck, trying to find a pulse. Edwin does the same with Garry's left wrist.

"*Se ha ido*," Edwin says gently. "*Se ha ido, hermanos*." He has gone, brothers.

Roman completes 30 more compressions and moves again toward Garry's head. "Let me try, please," I find myself saying as I crawl around to take Roman's place. Roman nods.

My left hand goes to Garry's forehead as I bring my ear to his nose and mouth. Not even the faintest sign of breath. I flash my headlamp into his open mouth to make sure his tongue is out of the way and then bring my mouth over the top of his, creating a tight seal around his cold, lifeless lips. The next 60 seconds are a series of well-intended but pointless gestures. After 18 hard pumps onto the sternum, which seems ready to crack, I realize we're trying to save a life that, as Edwin said, has already gone.

I sit back, and the six of us stare at one another in wide-eyed silence. From frenzied action to sober understanding of finality.

"*Adentro. Necesitamos moverlo adentro.*" The low rumble of Habin's voice breaks the silence. We need to move him inside.

In collective agreement, we once again set ourselves to motion. Edwin unrolls a woven blanket on the floor of Garry's hut and lights a few candles while the rest of us hoist Garry up and into the small, screened-in room. There is no sadness, remorse, or fear as we do these things. A larger force is at play right now, overriding any preprogrammed response we might expect to have. We're functioning as one organism now, doing what serves the highest good from one second to the next.

Animated and coursing with life only a few minutes ago, the flesh and bone that was once Garry now lays motionless in front of us. The candlelight plays off the contours of his face, occasionally tricking the eye. Was that a twitch? Did his hand just stir?

We sit in total silence, holding space for something infinitely larger than us. There is no visible interaction occurring, but the room is awash in an intensity that has us all entranced. There is a download in progress. Five minutes pass. Then ten.

Something is transpiring just above Garry's body. My eyes are transfixed by this, and it's overtly apparent that our awareness itself is playing some important role. We are witnessing something unwitnessable. The air in front of our faces is charged with energy emanating from the burly vessel that is stretched in front of us. Then, just like that, it lifts and is gone.

Garry is no longer here. This is not romanticizing or theorizing, but plainly obvious to everyone in the hut as the collective trance subsides instantly. I look at Roman and can't control the smile that is beginning to wash across my face. We've just witnessed a soul departing from its deceased body. This is something that many have experienced with their loved ones, but in this setting the miracle is so pronounced, so palpable, that everyone in our trusted circle is overcome with awe, gratitude, and . . . happiness?

The silence is broken by Roman, who sings an ícaro to send Garry's soul off to the ancestors. Once his song is complete, we begin to check in with one another, sharing what we witnessed and turning our focus to the practical question of "What now?"

The other patients will be awake in six hours, and many of those who are now in Garry's hut will need to be up and in service in five. Roman and I agree that he should use the satellite phone to call the coroner's office in Iquitos and arrange transport of Garry's body back to the port city in the morning.

"You guys all go get some rest; I'll stay here with Garry until sunrise." The words just seem to come out of my mouth without any decision on my part. A younger version of me would have been mortified to stay alone with a dead body in a little candlelit jungle hut, but that me no longer exists.

"Are you sure, brother? We can take turns or work in pairs if you'd like." Roman looks older somehow as he asks a question he already knows the answer to.

"I'll be fine. Really. See you all in the morning."

There is medicine in every challenging experience, and sitting cross-legged on the floor beside Garry's vessel as the rain falls around us is rewiring my understanding of my own mortality.

We Westerners shelter ourselves from death and dying at any expense. Even when it comes to our own loved ones, we tend to hire professional services to take care of the body and handle all the "arrangements." We're so fascinated by violence and murder on television and in the news, but when it comes to confronting death in our own lives, we are as scared as children.

The majority of people in the Western world identify with one of the major religions: Christianity, Judaism, or Islam. All of them hold in their core teachings the ultimate goal of living a selfless life of connectedness and service to others. Those who follow said guidelines are rewarded with some type of heavenly afterlife. The rules and reward are fairly straightforward, yet this same culture is plagued by an unwillingness to embrace aging and the ultimate death of our physical form.

I once heard a Buddhist mystic say, "The root of all fear is death, and the goal of all religions is to help humans to overcome that fear."

The candles burn low as the hours pass, ultimately extinguishing themselves. Darkness feels appropriate now, so, like Garry, I stay where I sit, holding final space for the deep-sea diver from Garibaldi.

■ ■ ■

Early the following morning, we arrange transport of Garry's body to the coroner's office in Iquitos. Roman and a few other locals accompany his remains for the 65-kilometer (40-mile) ride. There will be authorities to answer to, and the U.S. embassy will most likely be involved.

Once they've departed, Andrea and I visit each of the patients and ask them to meet us in the upper level of the maloka after they eat their breakfast. Most of them are already aware that something substantial happened last night.

An hour later, we sit in a circle on the floor of the vaulted room. The jungle around us is fully awake, humming, buzzing, and chirping in through the thin-screened walls.

"Many of you have already heard some news of what happened last night," I begin, "but I wanted to gather you here together so we could discuss it openly. For those of you who don't already know—" I choke up unexpectedly as the words fail to form in my throat.

Surprised and eerily fascinated by my floundering attempt to speak to the group, I try again. "Last night, Garry passed away." My eyes move involuntarily to the floor as I try to hold it together. *Why wasn't it this hard last night?*

And then the realization comes. I feel like I let them all down. I don't want them to second-guess their decision to come here. I don't want them to stop believing in the healing path.

"He was so happy here." Gretchen breaks the silence with a big smile as she speaks. "None of this got to him one bit. The man was made to be in the woods."

Jessica chimes in. "We bumped into each other on the trail the other day and he was radiating! He wasn't in any pain. He was feeling so good this past week. He told me all about the natural tendencies of one of the bees that we saw on a flower, and then we said goodbye."

The patients are all beaming and nodding in agreement as they share their final words about Garry, one by one. This is not what I was expecting, and it has me dumbfounded.

"I'm happy for him, because I know how he must have felt coming here. This opportunity showed up and gave him some hope, but he knew it was a long shot." Melinda's words come out wistfully. A fellow cancer patient, she is obviously sobered by the news, but her voice holds a deep reverence.

John, who just a few days ago yelled at one of the shamans for not letting him eat fruit for breakfast, speaks last. "He really loved it out here. He had nothing but positive things to say about everything and everyone here. I think he really had a chance to work through what he needed to work through in order to make the transition peacefully."

After all have spoken, I realize that I have underestimated these people who put so much faith in us. They might be struggling with an illness, but they are far from frail. These are some of the toughest individuals I've ever met. Most folks wouldn't want to brave the unknowns of this final jungle frontier in perfect health. The human beings sitting in front of me, and Garry as well, were willing to come all this way in a weakened state, knowing that it would be one of the hardest experiences of their lives.

Somehow in focusing on their weaknesses, I failed to fully acknowledge their strength. I promise myself it won't happen again.

"Are we still going to be having group meditation tonight and a San Pedro ceremony tomorrow?" It is Gretchen who asks, but everyone looks to me as if they have been wondering the same thing.

Coming into this room, I assumed that at least a few of the patients would want to go home immediately upon hearing the news of Garry. I was planning on opening that door to them and making arrangements for those who took me up on it. Now I see that this is the last thing that any of them are thinking about. *Put your game face on, Nick.*

"Absolutely. Group meditation tonight, and Roman will be back in the morning to begin preparing the maloka for San Pedro."

I stand up and walk to each patient to check in individually for a moment. Hugs are exchanged, and then the meeting is adjourned.

Heartened and a little shaken, I head back to the longhouse to make the dreaded call via satellite phone to Garry's emergency contact back in the States—his sister Susan.

■ ■ ■

There are moments in your life when you are stepping into such uncharted territory that you have no choice but to blindly stumble forward, suspending all inner dialogue. There is no right way to call a woman and tell her that her brother is dead. You just punch the numbers into the phone and let it unfold one second at a time.

Garry had told me that his sister thought he was crazy to come down here in his condition and that they had it out before he left. Don't think, just enter the numbers.

The standard ringing sound that you hear after dialing a number varies from country to country. Up in the States, it's a series of single-spaced rings, but in Peru it's a pair of droning beeps followed by a long silence.

Beep beep.

Beep beep.

"Hello, Nick?" The voice on the other end is clearly that of a woman, and her first two words are almost giggled rather than spoken. Do I have the right person, and how does she know it's me?

"Um, yes. Is this Susan?"

"Yes it is." Her voice quivers. "Is my brother dead?"

Tears flood my eyes for the first time since Garry left us, and I can't speak for a second. Sobbing, I garble into the speaker, "Yes, he is. I'm sorry, Susan."

She laughs a hearty laugh this time, now crying too. "Are you kidding me? He knew he had to be down there with you as soon as you walked into his house in Garibaldi a few months ago. He couldn't stop talking about you and the shamans—Nick this and

Roman that. He didn't want you to know it, but his condition worsened quickly in the month between your interview with him in Oregon and his trip down to the jungle. The doctors told him he only had a week to live the day before he left."

Susan's voice gets steadier as she goes on. "I told him not to go, that he should be here with his family when he passed, but my brother has been an outdoorsman his entire life and he wanted one last adventure. He'd never been to the Amazon before and really believed this was his last chance at getting better. He and I said goodbye before he left. I think we both knew it would be the last time I saw him."

"Wait a second . . ." I begin, not quite processing all I've just heard. "Garry never told us any of this. He had less than a week to live?"

"Yeah. He didn't want you to know. He thought you might not let him come. But he barely made it onto his plane because he needed so much assistance."

"Assistance? He was walking up and down the trails for the past week with no problem," I tell her. "He said he couldn't feel the tumors in his belly anymore and that he thought they were gone. I can't believe he never told me!"

She pauses for a moment, then says, more seriously, "There's much about Garry that nobody knows. The waters ran deep with that one." After a moment, she goes on. "Remember this: My brother wanted to be with you. He knew it was probably going to be his final few days of life, and he wanted to be down there with you and Roman. It sounds like he made the right choice."

■ ■ ■

The sun begins to slide below the forest canopy a few hours later. I'm sitting on the front steps of Hut 6 with Habin, who felt it would be a good idea to return to Garry's place and perform a smoke clearing.

"Sometimes a soul needs a little help to make the full transition. Let's ensure that Garry made a clean exit," Habin says as he lights a stick of palo santo. "I'll be back out in a few minutes."

The coca shaman enters the hut, barefoot, and stands in silence in the darkness of the 10-by-10-foot space for a good two minutes before making his way over to Garry's bed. He pulls up the mosquito net, holds the palo santo over the mattress, and begins to say a quiet prayer in Spanish. He then moves the smoldering incense over each surface in the room, watching the play of the smoke as he goes. His hand guides the tendrils into the seemingly empty pockets of air above the small table in the corner, then over the space on the floor where Garry's body lay last night.

Fifteen minutes later, Habin opens the screen door and sits down next to me on the steps. In the fading light, he opens his pouch, withdraws three coca leaves, arranges them into a kintu triad between forefinger and thumb, and says a small blessing. He bites into them, leaving only the stems in his fingertips, looks up at the sky, and begins to speak.

"What is death? What is life?

"Life without death has no meaning. Life doesn't exist without death. Wherever there is life, there is death. And we cannot hide from it.

"Death is a change, a process that is necessary for life. Those who live in the Western world have demonized it out of fear and ignorance. They believe there is something to be afraid of after death. But what is it? What is God? He is life itself. So they stay away from death, and by doing so they also stay away from life."

Habin draws three more coca leaves from his pouch, arranging them shiny side up, with stems pointing toward the ground. He studies them for a good minute and finally lets out a long breath through his nostrils. "It is done. He is no longer here."

Perhaps the reason that shamanism and indigenous medicine are spreading so quickly nowadays is because they hold basic, primal truths that resonate within all of us, the most powerful of these being the understanding that neither life nor death should be feared.

One thing we are guaranteed in this life is that there will be an end to our physical incarnation. Surrender is the only way forward. Surrender to the impermanence of this body, the impermanence of this emotion we are feeling right now, and the impermanence of any challenge we will ever face.

Chapter 9

◇◇◇◇◇◇◇◇◇◇◇◇◇◇

RELÁMPAGO

Thunder is good, thunder is impressive;
but it is lightning that does the work.

—MARK TWAIN

November 4, 2010
Loreto Province, Peru

It's around 9 P.M., and the team and I are wrapping up for the night. We're at the end of the third week of filming. The patients are going through plenty of breakdowns and breakthroughs, but morale is high. Garry's passing has galvanized the group, boosting determination and sense of purpose in both patients and healers.

It's been raining since sunrise, and we're busy cleaning gear, backing up footage, and planning for the following day. This has become our nightly ritual—a way to stay sharp and connect with one another before bed. In an environment like this, adhering to certain protocols during downtime helps to settle the mind and at least give the illusion of control over the highly unpredictable circumstances.

I'm peering over Brock's shoulder at a video clip he's analyzing when the walkie-talkie bleeps on. "Nick, please come to the maloka. It's important." Every one of us has grown wary of the abruptness of that device, especially at this hour of the night.

We sit in silence for a few moments. The tip-tap of falling droplets of water on the thatched roof overhead and wet breeze blowing in through the thin floor-to-ceiling screens of our longhouse tell me that I'm about to get wet. The rainy season is upon us, and the maloka is about a quarter mile deeper into the jungle.

I look over at Dan, who has resumed making notes in a Moleskine booklet, and he gives me a "Who knows?" shrug.

"Don't wait up for me," I say. I put on a poncho and walk down the creaky wooden steps to the cement slab foundation below. On go the oversize rubber mud boots, and out I walk into the night.

These rare moments away from the team, between one task and the next, have become vital for me. As I'm trudging along in the darkness through mud and plant life, my mind can turn off for a short while. There are no fires to put out, no decisions to be made, just me and the forest. We've been wet for a week now, so a little extra water is an easy trade-off for some solitude.

Fifteen minutes later, I'm splashing up an embankment and can now see the lights of the maloka. It's by far the tallest man-made structure for miles, at a whopping 35 feet high, casting long beams of light through the trees like a jungle lighthouse. Somebody must be waiting for me up in the attic.

The maloka is a two-level temple that is customary to most tribes in this neck of the jungle. The bottom level has no windows and the floor is fine white sand. This is where the ayahuasca ceremonies are held. The top level—or attic—of this particular structure is walled on all sides by windows with thin green screens, and its vaulted ceiling stretches up to the rafters and circular thatched roof above.

When candles are lit on the top floor at night, the octagonal structure turns into a towering lantern. And so it is as I approach, unsure of who or what is awaiting me.

I walk up the hand-hewn side steps that wrap around the building and peer through the screen door that is latched shut on the landing. I see the silhouettes of three people huddled around some candles inside.

I remove my boots and open the door. "Good evening, brother," Roman says as I enter. "Sorry to make you walk all the way out here in the rain, but the three of us are about to have a coca ceremony and we thought it would be good for you to join."

As I come closer, I see that the other two silhouettes belong to Edwin and Habin, the mysterious shaman who seems to be revealing more of his supernatural skills with each passing day. Rumor has it that as a young man, Habin wandered into Manu National Park—a large stretch of the Amazon wilderness and home to some of the last uncontacted tribes—and wasn't seen or heard from for 10 years. He emerged in his mid-30s with some serious healing knowledge (among other things) and now works primarily with coca and mapacho, Amazonian tobacco.

Habin's demeanor is grave as he stares at me in the candlelight.

"Have you ever sat in a coca ceremony before?" His Spanish is rapid and his accent is totally different from what I'm used to, but his question is clear enough.

"No," I answer. This will be my first. "But I've been chewing a lot of coca during the day while we work," I add, trying to be helpful.

"A coca ceremony is an entirely different thing. With a proper ceremony, this plant will show you an entirely different side of itself. We sit, we chew, we smoke mapacho, and we share stories of who we are and how we came to be. Make no mistake, this isn't a time for idle chatter. We share from our hearts. Otherwise we listen."

I'm beginning to lose track of him. My Spanish is serviceable when it comes to one-on-one communication where the speaker slows down to accommodate my language handicap. But a more rapid exchange like this one is beyond my ability.

Seeing my poorly disguised confusion, Habin glances at Roman, then back at me. The two exchange some quick remarks in abbreviated slang about the current stage I'm at with the local dialect.

Habin motions toward an open patch of floor, indicating that I should park myself there.

Don't worry about it, I tell myself. *Just relax and make yourself comfortable. We're apparently going to be here for a while.*

The coca shaman digs into his satchel and pulls out a small mesa blanket that is intricately woven with multicolored fabric. Next, he produces a large bag from which he removes a generous handful of coca leaves, spreading them across the mesa while saying some quiet words to himself.

He motions to Roman, inviting him to partake first—a clear sign of respect for the other shaman, and then Edwin, who gently selects a few leaves with the discernment of a collector examining stamps or coins. And finally, I am invited in.

Ceremonies like this can last for five or six hours, depending on the occasion and the shaman who is holding them. The first 10 or so leaves that we pack into our mouths will be followed by hundreds more before the night is over.

"*Hallpay kusinchis*," Habin says to the three of us as he blows on three perfectly formed leaves positioned between his thumb and index finger. Closing his eyes, he says a few more words under his breath before biting the leaves off so that only the stems remain.

Chew, chew, chew. Once the leaves are pulverized by your teeth, you maneuver them with your tongue over to the side of your mouth, between molars and cheek. That's where the leaves stay as you pack more in and let the enzymes in your saliva extract the active constituents from them.

"Edwin, tell us a story about yourself." Habin speaks through a mouthful of coca as he continues to select more leaves from the pile and pack them in.

"About me? Hmm . . . Well, the story of how I met Roman is pretty interesting—right, Roman?" Roman nods, and Edwin begins to tell us of his first encounter with the shaman and how unlikely it was that their paths should cross.

As usual, I'm fully able to understand the conversation until Edwin begins to share some intricate emotions regarding his upbringing, the way his mother treated him growing up, and some conflicts he still had with his brother.

I know I'm completely lost when he pauses and makes a parenthetical comment that must hold some scandalous backstory and the two other shamans interject their own remarks with lowered voices. Apparently Edwin's tale has reached some juicy climax that I am completely unaware of.

Damn. I can't stand when this happens. One of the worst feelings in the world for a documentary filmmaker and human being, is when a language barrier prevents you from participating or at least understanding an important conversation. These three invited me here to be part of a special counsel meeting of sorts, and here I am, clueless as to what is being discussed.

I sit, nodding falsely at them while they speak, while I continue to stuff more and more coca into my cheeks—the only thing I can think to do to show my enthusiasm.

After about 10 minutes of feeling like a buffoon and wallowing silently in being on the outside of this intimate session, I decide I'm just going to give in to the experience and act the way I feel, rather than playing along. I lean back on my elbows, find a cushion under the window behind me, and lie down, staring at the weblike eaves above me.

The conversation pauses for a second while I do this, as the three obviously take note of my shift away from the group, but it starts right up again a moment later.

The juices from the wad of coca begin to trickle down my throat as I listen to the infinite drops of rain exploding off the leaves, limbs, and mud outside. The bitter juice is beginning to numb my gums. The wind is starting to pick up in the surrounding forest, blowing wet air through the screen wall that separates us from the jungle.

Something in the air is changing.

I hear the faintest rumble underneath the pitter-patter and rustle of wind through trees. And then another.

I love storms.

Another 15 minutes pass. My three companions continue their lively discussion, and I remain a satellite on the outskirts of the circle, but completely content to be. I can't tell if it's the coca or simply being in the presence of these shamans, but I am filled with a sort of electric giddiness, and the feeling is intensifying with every minute.

A flash and crackle from above brightens the forest to the north of us for a few seconds. I've never seen lightning in the jungle before. Oceans of rain, yes, but never lightning. It's getting closer.

Habin is now in the middle of recounting one of his long journeys up the Manu River, where he almost died of starvation after days of wandering through the jungle, lost and without supplies.

His voice lowers as he speaks about a specific night, when he thought all was lost as he huddled under a large lapuna tree on a riverbank for warmth. "I was trying to will myself to sleep when I began to hear the most beautiful singing carried on the breeze from upriver. I got up and began to stumble through the forest in the direction of this heavenly sound, seeing my way by the light of the moon. As I came around a bend in the bank, I saw before me something that still gives me chills to this day. A mermaid (*una sirena*) sitting right there on a rock in the middle of the river—"

"A mermaid! Come on. Really? Like a real one, or a vision of a mermaid? Have either of you ever heard of anything like this?" I speak out of turn almost involuntarily. The locals tell tales about jungle mermaids, but I've never heard of an actual interaction with one.

"No, it was a real mermaid, my friend. Just ask the locals, even in this region. Foreigners think these stories are myth, but the native people know they are—" Habin breaks off. "Wait a second— look who decided to join the conversation!" Roman, Habin, and Edwin grin at me across the cluster of candles between us.

"What? Oh . . ." Somehow the garbled code that the other three have been speaking is 85 percent comprehensible now. "I've never been able to understand half of these words."

"Coca is powerful that way. It opens up new pathways for communication, internally and externally. You are now experiencing its full effect."

Rumble. CRACK.

While Habin is speaking, the forest lights up around us. A tree that couldn't be more than 100 yards away is hit by lightning and falls to the jungle floor with a loud thud.

Our heads snap around involuntarily in the direction of the strike. "That one was really close," Edwin observes.

Roman's eyes are wide open. "Not to worry. This maloka is only half the height of the trees outside. We are safe here."

Habin turns and faces me square on. "Now that we can understand each other, I'd like to hear more about who you are and what your intention is for this documentary that we all seem to be wrapped up in."

Oh. This coca ceremony is really another shamanic test. Here goes.

"Well," I begin, "I've been involved in two other films to date that follow patients who are trying to heal themselves using a specific natural method. While we were filming them, a few of our experts made mention of shamanism. I followed the bread crumb trail, and that led me here."

Seems logical enough to me, but Habin doesn't seem totally satisfied. I try again.

"My mission in this world, as I see it, is to show people that they are more powerful than they realize. So many folks are sick and looking for answers, with only Western medicine to turn to—which is failing them miserably. I healed myself of chronic migraine headaches five years ago using natural medicine, and I'm on a quest of sorts to bring ancient healing methods to the people who need them most."

"That is all very interesting, but you wouldn't be sitting here with us right now just because of a natural healing quest." Habin glances at Roman, then back at me. His eyes move down to the pile of coca leaves on the mesa blanket in front of him and stop, and he stares at something in their configuration for about 30 seconds while we sit in silence. He nods, inhaling a deep breath through his nostrils, then exhales.

"*Bueno.* Okay, Nick, can you tell me of any significant life-changing events that occurred when you were 16?"

Sixteen. That's random. Well, actually, that was a pretty bad year in the life of Nick. All those car accidents, and the other stuff.

"Well, I'm not sure if this is what you're referring to, but right after I got my driver's license I got in five car accidents. And one boat accident. I wasn't really hurt in any of them, but the boat accident involved a high-speed crash into and over a small island, and the police said it was a miracle that we survived."

Roman chuckles, shaking his head. "They still let you have your license after the first two accidents? Remind me never to let you drive, *hermano.*"

"I haven't had a car accident since—knock on wood."

Habin's voice cuts through the air. "You're not telling us everything. What else happened to you in that year?"

Jeez. What does this guy want from me? I thought the car and boat accident thing was pretty substantial. "Um . . . let me think. Such a long time ago, you know?"

The rain is starting to pound on the roof of the maloka. A loud rumble comes from somewhere above us.

Oh yeah, *that.* But does that really count as substantial?

"What is the word for lightning in Spanish again?" I ask Roman in English.

"*Relámpago,*" he answers.

When Habin hears this word, the coca chewing stops and eyebrows rise.

"When I was 16, I might have been partially struck by lightning," I say hesitantly. "I was standing outside during a storm for some reason, and, well, lightning split the tree next to me in half."

"Relámpago? You're sure you understand the meaning of this word?" The coca shaman leans toward me as he inquires.

"Yeah, lightning. BOOM! From the sky—electricity like the one that hit that tree a few minutes ago. I was really dumb to be outside that day. I could have died."

Habin turns to Roman. "Did you know about this?"

"No. This is news to me as well." Roman's eyes are a mystery as he responds to his friend. Something serious is going on, but I have no idea what it is.

"In the Andes Mountains, an encounter with lightning is one of the most significant rites of passage on the shamanic path. Were you aware of this?" Habin has apparently extracted the tidbit he was looking for from my teenage years. Pretty impressive that he was able to pinpoint it with such accuracy just by looking at a few scattered leaves.

"No, I didn't know that," I say, still wondering what's going on.

Habin goes on to explain that in the Andes, a *pampamisayoc*, or highland healer-priest, can only become an *altomisayoc*, the highest level of shaman, if chosen by Pachamama herself. The word *altomisayoc* means "chosen by the beam" in Quechua. He looks up into the rafters, toward the thunder rumbling in the sky above us.

"This happened to you when you were 16, and you magically find yourself here with us. This is no coincidence. Please tell us more about your encounter with the relámpago."

■ ■ ■

Lightning (lit´ning) n.

1. An abrupt, discontinuous natural electric discharge in the atmosphere.

2. Informal: A sudden, usually improbable stroke of fortune.

Have you ever done something that in retrospect turned out to be a really stupid idea? Of course you have; you're a human being. Well, I did something really dumb when I was 16 years old that changed the course of my life forever.

It was late afternoon in June of 1994 and I had just broken up with my high school sweetheart, which was a very big deal. Not only was she my first girlfriend, but she also single-handedly, through her own popularity, elevated me from a quiet nobody to a somewhat conversational somebody in the course of just six months—no small feat. But after about a year and a half of young love, it just wasn't working out, and we decided, rather emotionally, to go our separate ways.

On the official day of breakup, there was something very beautiful happening weather-wise. If you've lived in the northeastern United States, you're no stranger to the magnificent thunderstorms that roll in periodically throughout the summer, seemingly out of nowhere, darkening the skies on a hot and humid day. Towering cumulonimbus clouds close in upon one another, temporarily turning day into night, as drops of water descend from the heavens to meet rather abruptly with blistering-hot pavement, scorched lawns, and the heads of disappointed golfers.

It was that kind of afternoon, and this particular weather pattern mimicked my inner climate of heartbreak so closely that I felt compelled to walk outside in the middle of the torrential downpour that was raging outside my house.

Moved by the appropriateness of it all, I went into my garage and grabbed my boom box radio (kind of a 1980s Run-DMC knockoff), popped in a mixtape Kim had given me, and walked out with deeply satisfying dramatic flair into the quickly flooding driveway of my suburban home.

The raindrops were huge and many and cold, but they felt good as they hit my head and shoulders and quickly drenched my shirt. The sky was rumbling overhead, the clouds morphing and undulating as they moved quickly by. Flashes of lightning danced along the ridge of trees that delineated our neighborhood from the next one over, each followed by a quick clap of thunder.

When I was little my father had taught me how to track the distance of a lightning bolt by counting the seconds between the flash in the clouds and the audible crack and rumble that came after. We'd sit for an hour at a time watching the sky and tracking the storms, waiting for fire in the sky.

I stood there in my driveway, just feet away from Tower Road, so named because it led to the highest point in town, during one of the strongest thunderstorms we would have all year. I was about

15 feet from a very tall oak tree when the unthinkable happened (well, thinkable to any rational person, but not thinkable to me at the time).

BANG.

I remember a blinding flash of white light that consumed everything in my field of vision. Perfectly timed with this white-out was a deafening sound, like you would hear from the guns on a warship, but louder and more electric. If you've ever heard a high-voltage transformer explode, that's about the same noise.

Now, I wish I could say that in those moments immediately following the lightning strike I had some deeply meaningful spiritual experience of oneness or saw my grandmother (who had just passed) in a near-death vision, but I cannot.

I do think I peed a little, but I was too drenched from the rain to know for sure.

I must have been out for at least a few minutes. When I eventually came to, I was very wet, very cold, and had a splitting headache. The rain had lightened a bit. The blacktop around me was now covered in leaves and splintered wood. The old oak tree that had stood right next to me moments before had been split right down the middle—half of the tree still stood erect and the other half had been blown to bits all over my yard and self.

The now me would be floored and humbled by an experience like this. But the accident-prone, bad-luck 16-year-old me immediately went into disaster-management mode. My mom and dad would be home from work soon, and if they found out that I had been outside during a lightning storm, under one of the tallest trees on our property no less, well, it wouldn't be good.

Cleanup on aisle ME.

Fighting an amplified gravitational pull beneath me, I drew myself up, brain still throbbing, ears ringing, and hightailed it into my house. Reality continued to spin as I took a shower, definitely did not do my homework (that part wasn't unusual), and put together a convincing story to tell my parents when they got home. Lying was an art that I had perfected early on in life, and it served me well that day.

Looking back on it now, it seems crazy to think that in all the discussions my family later had around that storm and the split oak tree, I never confessed that I was standing right next to it at the time of impact. I guess I didn't trust anyone back then, aside from the freckly-faced 16-year-old I had just broken up with.

． ． ．

"So you have been on this path since you were 16. And are you training to be a shaman's apprentice with Roman, in addition to making this film?" Habin's face shows little emotion as he turns to me, aside from slightly raised eyebrows. It's easy to see why people are intimidated by this man.

"No, that's not my path. I'm here to document this wisdom and share it with those who are seeking more. I'm not a shaman."

"He is sitting here in the jungle, chewing coca and speaking a language he didn't know just two hours ago, and now he's telling us a tale of being struck by lightning. Brother, forgive me for jumping to conclusions."

I'm not a shaman, and I have no desire to be. But it's eerily reassuring that I've been on this path longer than I was aware of.

EVERYTHING IS MEDICINE

There is a principle I learned from the shamans that I've retooled, souped up, and morphed into my own code for walking the sacred path, not in spite of but *at the hands of* the modern world around us. It's based on a three-word bit of knowledge from the Amazon: *Everything is medicine*.

I'm not saying you should take a spoonful of Elmer's Glue to cure your cold. It's more figurative than that. What native healers are getting at is that everything that happens to you in this life, every single moment, good or bad, has a lesson to teach you.

If you don't take anything else away from this book, I would consider my job complete if you just absorbed and integrated this one understanding. It will transform the world around you from a place of good, bad, and eh to an immeasurably rich incubator for personal evolution.

Everything that has ever happened to you and will ever occur around you can be seen through one of two lenses: medicine or poison. It's totally your choice, but your mind-set will determine which choice you make. It's in keeping with an ancient observation by the Greek philosopher Epictetus, "It's not what happens to you, but how you react to it that matters."

There is an overall approach to healing disease in the jungle that I think might interest you.

Many tribes of the Upper Amazon basin consider diseases to be "mothers." When someone falls ill and begins to undergo their healing journey, it is believed by the shamans that the spirit of that disease, or mother, has become pregnant with this individual. During this gestation period, the mother has much to teach through her effects on the body and mind: the physical weakness, the pain, the need to rely on others, to *trust* in others, to let go of our hold on what we expected this life to look like, to confront our own mortality.

These opportunities for surrender and humility are all packaged perfectly within a serious disease and presented as a lesson for the soul.

The shamans teach that if we humans can walk with the disease mother, with eyes wide open, and learn the hidden lessons she has to offer, we will be reborn from her womb as a healthy, more spiritually harmonious being, taking with us the boatload of wisdom gleaned from the experience.

Those who instead close up and resist the disease, shutting themselves off from the experience, may very well be reborn, but onto a different plane of existence—the next life. Every challenge in life can be looked at in this way. Either medicine (mother) or poison.

Shamans don't just decide that they'd like to heal people for a living. Most true shamans have been through their own involuntary rite of passage, something that caught the attention of the elders when they were in their youth. This usually involves a miraculous recovery from a deathly illness, or literally dying and coming back from a flatline state.

When medicine men or women speak to their patients about embracing their illness, surrendering to it, and learning the lessons it has to teach, this is not a theory they picked up from a textbook. It is how they themselves survived and became the healers they are now.

As Romanian historian Mircea Eliade wrote, "The primitive magician, the medicine man or shaman is not only a sick man, he is, above all, a sick man who has been cured, who has succeeded in curing himself."

This shamanic lens for examining and overcoming illness can also be applied to any challenge that we encounter as we walk through this life. Medicine folk approach everything that life brings them with full openness to the wisdom it holds. Like our immune systems, our souls and psyches become stronger and more adaptable through exposure to external attack.

In this way, shamans and their pupils are constantly strengthening and stretching the inner muscles of awareness, unflinchingly witnessing all that unfolds in order to learn and evolve.

What challenge in your life, illness or otherwise, is tugging at your sleeve, asking to be reexamined as a catalyst for your spiritual growth?

Chapter 10

◇◇◇◇◇◇◇◇◇◇◇◇◇◇◇

GRANDFATHER

Walking, I am listening to a deeper way. Suddenly all my
ancestors are behind me. Be still they say. Watch and listen.
You are the result of the love of thousands.

—LINDA HOGAN, CHICKASAW NATION WRITER

November 11, 2010
Larapata, Peru

It's high noon, and the jungle is hot outside the large maloka. Every one of the patients is gathered in a large circle on the top level of the wooden structure, spaced around the inner perimeter against the windows.

We are moments away from starting a San Pedro ceremony. Referred to by many names, such as *huachuma*, *mescalito*, and *Grandfather*, the Andean cactus is thought of as being inherently masculine, whereas ayahuasca embodies the divine feminine. Just looking at the phallic shape of San Pedro, it's easy to see why this association exists.

The effects and ritual around the two medicines fall neatly into these two gender archetypes as well. Where ayahuasca drains one of strength, beckoning the user to surrender to the unknown realms of the cosmos, San Pedro floods one with power, tugging at the journeyer to sense the fullness of his or her body. Grandma is experienced in the dark, while San Pedro is most often worked with during the day, which lines up with other traditions, like Chinese mysticism, where darkness is associated with the feminine and light is associated with the masculine. Yin and yang are a prime example.

Scientifically speaking, the Andean cactus contains phenethylamine alkaloids, most notably mescaline, that produce altered thinking processes, a changed sense of time and self-awareness, and both closed- and open-eyed visual phenomena.

Grandmother Ayahuasca, believed by many to be the counterpart of San Pedro, has opened up most of our guests to sides of themselves they didn't know were there. Some of them, including Gretchen, have revisited extremely traumatic events from their past that they had effectively hidden from themselves for decades, not realizing that the scarring was contributing to the illness they're now working through.

San Pedro, on the other hand, has been a mixed bag for the patients. Some have encountered extreme spiritual breakthroughs with Grandfather, while others have felt either nothing at all or extreme disorientation followed by a sense of disconnectedness and confusion. The assortment of contrasting expressions on the faces around me are a clear reflection of who has experienced what.

Roman is sitting cross-legged in his usual spot in the maloka, at 12 o'clock, smiling warmly as he unties his medicine bundle and begins to place vessels, stones, and other ceremonial objects on a traditional mesa blanket laid out before him.

"This has been quite a process for everyone, and we are honored to be helping you through it," he begins. "We have been working with mostly Amazonian traditions for these first few weeks and have had only one San Pedro ceremony so far. Today we will be journeying much deeper into this ancient Andean ceremony.

"San Pedro is one of the most sacred plants of the high Andes, but it works much differently from ayahuasca. We can't simply ingest it and wait for the experience to begin. We must make certain efforts and meet San Pedro midway."

The past four weeks or so have been a roller coaster of ups and downs for each of our guests. As they have gone deeper into themselves and become more attuned to what one of the shamans calls their "primordial essence," new emotional blocks have come up. These phantoms aren't pretty at first glance, but each of them is starting to see these for what they are: sentinels at the gates of transcendence.

One day there is a new spiritual or physical breakthrough; the next there is a revelation of a deeper wound that needs to be worked through. Like peeling the layers of an onion, there seems to be more work to do as you make your way to the center.

"The purpose of working with the plant medicines," Roman says, "is to voluntarily increase the intensity of any thoughts or emotions we're experiencing so they can be worked through and dissolved. Once the spirit of San Pedro is upon us, we will be working with specific practices that will help us see through the facade and recognize our true essence."

With that, drumming starts and we are called one by one to receive our spoonful of sun-dried huachuma, which we quickly wash down with water once it hits our tongues. There's no escaping the taste, a combination of hand soap and licking a battery, with an undertone of classroom chalk. The last time I had it, it was in liquid form, so this is a substantial improvement.

We go around the circle three times, taking a healthy helping with every pass.

The effects of San Pedro typically take about 30 minutes to set in, and in the interim there are some common bodily sensations that take hold—dry mouth, nausea, a need to release the bowels, and sometimes dizziness. To work through these initial effects, Roman takes us through a series of movement meditations to help circulate the energy and ground any discomfort we might be feeling—mostly a mixture of qigong and traditional Amazonian breathing exercises.

Midstretch in the white crane posture, my eyes fall on Nicola, who is reclining in a hammock that is strung over her usual place in the circle.

Her expression, which is usually hard to read, has changed completely as she swings in the warm breeze with a peaceful smile on her face. The delicate facial muscles around her mouth are starting to work again. It's something that most of us take for granted, the use of these muscles that help us express complex emotions without words; for Nicola, it was one of the many losses of function that she experienced from her illness.

She has been working very closely with Habin, now known by the patients as "the motorcycle shaman" because of his preferred mode of transportation, and the past few days have been pure transformation for her.

Their work together began with a few one-on-one meetings, similar to a psychotherapy session, during which Habin asked a number of questions (via a translator) to get an idea of what her history and daily life were like at home. It took Habin hours, but Nicola finally began to open up about the dark personal life that had been brewing long before the terrible car accident and onset of Parkinson's symptoms a few years ago.

It all began with one well-placed question from the shaman: "What is the most important thing to you in this world?"

"That's simple," said Nicola immediately. "My boys. I would do anything for Nat and Brian. It's why I'm here in the jungle right now—to get healthy again so I don't lose them."

She continued, detailing how her once loving husband had turned abusive in the year leading up to her car crash, and how her marriage had fallen apart. Nicola was left disabled in the wake of the accident, with temporarily limited motor function. Her now ex-husband had moved in on the kids. He'd taken her to court, attempting to gain full custody of the boys by claiming that she was a danger to them and unfit to be their guardian. She had no choice but to spend the little money she had and all of her energy fighting to keep her children—in addition to trying to find answers to the tremors that were beginning to take over her body.

My mouth begins to water as the San Pedro starts to kick in, followed by a rumbling in my bowels.

Keep breathing like Roman is. Let the stretch in each pose wring the stagnation from your system. Don't let your body tense up.

After quelling this wave of biological shakiness, my awareness falls back on the glowing woman in the hammock.

After his second session with Nicola, Habin called a meeting with the other shamans and me. He told us he had seen her exact situation in another Parkinson's patient about a year earlier outside the city of Lima. He had traveled there to visit a man who had suddenly begun experiencing tremors after his wife divorced him and won full custody of the children. Within a year, this man had gone from a healthy 40-year-old to a frail, tremoring shell of who he once was. He was desperate and told Habin he would do anything it took to get his health back and be a part of his children's lives.

A few days ago, Habin, Roman, and I were eating breakfast next to the glowing clay oven outside the kitchen hut when Habin brought up the idea of using a sacred but dangerous jungle plant to help Nicola. "In cases like this, there is one plant that can be highly effective. It is one of the most powerful plants in the jungle, and one of the few that can heal illnesses like this. It's called *toé*."

"Toé?" Roman looked at me, knowing that I was aware of how dangerous it is. "Are you sure that is a good idea?"

A few years earlier, I had come across the night bloomer in an old Harvard ethnobotanical text from the late Richard Evans Schultes and had marked it down as a definite no-no. Although toé holds volumes of promising medicinal applications, it's extremely hallucinogenic and has been known to cause irreversible psychological trauma and sometimes death. It's one of the most powerful power plants of the Amazon.

According to the shamans in this neck of the woods, the ceremonial plants used in indigenous cultures can be divided into two categories—teacher plants and power plants. Teacher plants deliver very intense effects and can take you to your existential edge, but there is always a way out. It is believed that these teacher plants possess a benevolent spirit that is always watching out for you during the experience, to make sure you make it back safely. Ayahuasca and San Pedro would fall into the category of teacher plants. They are powerful medicines that should be approached with ultimate respect and caution, but within each of them is a built-in ally—Grandmother and Grandfather.

Power plants, on the other hand, do not always allow you to leave a bread trail back to this reality and can be extremely dangerous if used incorrectly. They should be taken only by those with years of experience with plant medicines or by patients under the supervision of a trusted plant maestro. They have the ability to heal but can also lead to permanent dissociation, blindness, and death. Power plants include vilca, mapacho, and toé.

"I feel it's her best option," said Habin between mouthfuls of papaya and quinoa. "She has deep patterns around her children and husband that are making her rigid. Toé will help her dissolve this and see her life for what it really is. I used this to help the gentleman from Lima, and he was cured of his tremors in two months. Now he is able to be a good father to his children.

"Like him, Nicola must learn to be calm with her children and help them without becoming a slave to them," he continued. "Devoting her life to her family led her to follow a very fixed path. Our job now is to free her from that."

The risk of toé was immense, and we explained this to Nicola, but she adamantly wanted to try it, insisting that she had begun to make significant progress under Habin's care. It was a hard decision, especially after losing Garry a week before, but I found myself trying to persuade Roman to let her do it.

"These people are here because it's their last shot at getting better," I argued. "Who are we to tell them no?" At length he gave in.

The shaman and his patient spent two long nights in the throes of deep ceremony with toé, or angel trumpet, left in complete solitude—no visitors allowed. The morning after their first ceremony, Nicola lay in her bed, motionless, and stared up at the rafters for the remainder of the day. The following night, she came back into herself and again drank the toé brew. When Roman and

I checked in on them the second morning, Nicola sat right up in bed unassisted, put her feet on the floor, and stood to bid us a warm "Good morning!"

The initial shock at seeing this person fully animated with almost no trace of her Parkinson's symptoms was immense. Roman looked at Habin, who remained seemingly indifferent to the transformation that had taken place, and then turned to Nicola, asking her how she was feeling.

"I feel much better. Obviously!" She chuckled, then elaborated. "I've seen some very interesting things over the past few nights. Some visitors have come and gone, and Habin helped me work with them. They seemed so real when they appeared outside my hut. I was wide awake."

The woman sitting before us was now speaking in an elegant English accent. Her tremors and clenching had been so extreme in the timbre and cadence of her voice that her natural way of talking had been indistinguishable until now. As if they had thawed after a long freeze, her jaw and tongue now worked fluidly, producing a melodic and unmistakably British lilt.

"Maestro, what do you think of her progress?" Habin asked. "It looks like she is responding well to the treatment." Roman peered across the shady room at his friend with a rare look of surprise. Habin, for all he had accomplished with his patient, showed no sign of self-satisfaction or smugness.

"There is much left to be done," he said simply.

The universe has a funny way of bringing you to your edge. You draw a line in the sand, and the cosmic powers that be have a charming way of nudging you toward and over it, constantly showing you how futile your effort to control and shape your reality is.

We took a huge risk letting Nicola take one of the deadliest medicines in the jungle, but looking at her now as she smiles in her hammock, it's clear that we made the right decision.

■　■　■

Three hours later, I'm sitting knee to knee with Juan, our patient with depression, staring directly into his pupils. Everyone else in the circle has paired off as well in an eye-gazing ritual that Roman often deploys during mescalito ceremony.

They say the eyes are a gateway to the soul, and yet we humans go out of our way to bar entry into that portal. Most of us have a knee-jerk aversion to staring directly into someone's eyes for a prolonged period, even our lovers'. Living in New York City, you're lucky to make eye contact of any kind with the people you encounter.

During Roman's San Pedro ceremonies, each participant rotates to a new partner every 10 minutes, and pairs gaze into each other's eyes until everyone has seen everyone else.

Each gaze usually starts with the normal precursor to intimate interaction—smiles, giggles, awkward aversion, discomfort, sweaty palms. Eyes adjust, lids widen and narrow, facial muscles twitch, and bodily posture shifts to accommodate the pupil-lock. Then, like clockwork, things begin to shift.

Once the two tunnels of awareness are engaged, the gazer begins to lose him or herself, becoming a witness to a closed-circuit consciousness loop and the truth it radiates. The flesh around the two portals often shifts, becoming a variety of countenances, patterns.

The emotional response to each pairing can vary, some ending in dumbfounded laughter at the information that was just transmitted, some ending in tears of realization that we are all one— that judgment of other people is in fact a judgment of yourself.

As Juan and I sit, a single message seems to be transmitted over and over in my mind:

To the extent that we're all connected, the negative thoughts we hold toward one another and simultaneously toward ourselves are the equivalent of magic spells or curses that inflict damage until they are cleared.

Consciousness is the only cure.

We're souls from the same origin, encapsulated in flesh and bone. We strive for separation and private property on the physical plane, but it keeps us from understanding how powerful we are as a collective. Judgment of others comes from judgment of self.

These patients have put their full faith in me, and I've allowed the perceived burden of this responsibility to keep me detached. But healing doesn't happen in a vacuum, and this separation may actually be inhibiting my and their experience. What happens if I just give over to the experience and stop creating so many rules for myself?

"Okay," says Roman suddenly. "It's time for us to switch again. Thank your partner for the experience, and find your next pairing."

Juan nods and closes his eyes. I thank him and give him a hug.

Download received.

I glance up to see John, our prostate cancer patient, staring with wide-eyed terror into the smiling eyes of his gaze-partner Gretchen. The exercise is over, but the two are interlocked in a transmission that my gut tells me is too deep for me to even begin to contemplate. A minute later she leans forward and gives him a big hug. The look of disturbance on his long face is replaced with one of sadness and gratitude. His eyes glass over and then close. Something is happening inside of our man from Australia.

■ ■ ■

Final beams of sunlight are bouncing off and through the tattered burlap curtain that separates the toilet stall that I am currently occupying from the forest outside. An hour ago, San Pedro began to feel like Grandma in my stomach and I left the circle with comical but very real urgency, walking away hastily, then stopping to regain my intestinal composure, looking up at the group, waving to let them know I was okay, and then continuing to awkwardly make my way toward the side door.

I'm now seated on the bowl in the throes of an uncomfortable but satisfying plant purge.

Through a hole in rough fabric, I see the ceremonial maloka looming against the wide, cloudless sky, its thatched steeple reaching almost as high as the palm trees that surround it. The *energía* of San Pedro is in my musculature, in my head, in my throat and ears, coursing through my arms and legs, running through my fingertips and the bottoms of my feet.

It is said that the mescalito medicines give one great power, but if improperly used during ceremony, they can disorient, overwhelm, and terrify. The senses are heightened, the awareness even more keen, making me want to get on all fours and prowl the forests like a puma. Sometimes I do, but today is different.

Sitting with all the patients in ceremony and working to dissolve our illusion in a sacred communal setting has me feeling soft, grateful, and somehow vulnerable.

My ears key in on a new sound high up in the maloka, the ringing of strings being plucked over the loose rhythm of a hand drum. Roman's odd little guitar is the only creation capable of emitting such an out-of-tune yet entrancing melody.

Looking up through the trees and into the screened chamber, I can see the silhouettes of half the people in the room, mostly sitting or lounging on the floor. But there is a tall and slender man-shape off to the side, standing upright and moving—or flailing—in an uncontrolled manner to the music.

Here we go.

A few minutes later I'm climbing the steps back up to the wooden octagon, the melody becoming louder and faster as I approach. In all honesty, I can't tell whether the music is actually being played at a higher tempo and decibel level, or if Grandpa San Pedro is playing tricks on me.

The door creaks open unsubtly, giving way to an interior that is now awash with the warm glow of candlelight. As I enter, I look across the room to Roman, who is in a state of focus as his fingers move over the strings of his peculiar dwarf guitar. His eyes are trained on the spectacled body that has come alive across the room.

It's John, and he is crouched like a gargoyle with both hands stretched in front of himself, each finger shaking and recoiling at impossible intervals. His mouth is hanging open as he stares ahead, occasionally muttering to someone or something that isn't visible from where I'm standing.

Ever so slowly, he begins to rise from his squatting position, face and animated hands continuing their communication with the unknown. A minute later, he is standing fully erect and his hands have traveled down to his sides. His expression is still blank, his eyes a mystery behind the glimmer of firelight on glass lenses.

The disorienting, seemingly directionless music slips into a faster tempo, shimmying up and down in a hypnotic loop. Roman is singing an ícaro, but the sound coming from the shaman's lips has the rasp and labored delivery of an 80-year-old man.

Roman's voice and music are coaxing something out of John that is uncomfortable to watch but impossible not to. The man is walking on some other plane, encountering new parts of himself, rediscovering the full range of motion and expression of his physical form. He is electric.

I've seen something like this before. In the bazaars of Morocco, I once saw a Berber snake charmer play a similarly hypnotic melody to coax a cobra out of a basket and out into the open air.

And like that, the music stops.

Nobody speaks, and the evening sounds of the jungle begin to interject and regain hold of the space. All eyes are on John. Supporting, not judging. This is ceremony.

Swaying slightly in the night air, John looks down at one of his trembling hands and brings it up to his face. He inspects it for a few moments as if it isn't attached to his body—turning it frontward and backward, waving it back and forth, and with a look of realization coming across his face, stilling his animated fingers.

He looks across the room at Roman and then at all of us and nods, closing his eyes and bringing his hands up to his heart. His eyes remain closed and his head bowed as he lowers himself into a crouch again, hands moving into a self-embrace as he begins to rock himself backward and forward on bare feet.

Roman rises, crosses the octagon, and crouches down too, mirroring John's posture. There is nothing comical about this. We are witnessing a shaman deep in his work.

Sensing Roman in front of him, John's head lifts slightly and his eyes open.

"Thank you, Roman."

Roman brings his hands up to the sides of John's cranium and pulls it toward his own, until the two men are touching foreheads. Eyes closed, he begins to speak quickly and indecipherably, rocking back and forth.

The two are in a momentary trance together before the shaman slowly leans back and looks into the other man's eyes.

"Yeah?" Roman asks.

"Yeah."

The two embrace and begin to laugh.

I get up and begin to move awkwardly toward the exit again, stopping mid-octagon and bending involuntarily to hunch, staring downward, hoping the content of my bowels stays put.

Roman looks up, noticing my predicament.

"Brother, is there something of interest on the floor there?" This elicits a smattering of giggles from John and others.

"Not yet."

EYE GAZING

The eyes are the windows to the soul.

—UNKNOWN

We have these two orbs in our head through which we see and recognize the reality around us. They are capable of distinguishing the most minute details of our surroundings and interpreting the slightest discrepancy in another's countenance to distinguish mood and intention.

And yet, we rarely turn our pupils directly upon another set. It's uncomfortable to make eye contact with someone for too long in normal conversation, but what is the source of that unease? What don't you want to show that person? What don't you want that person to show you?

As we often find on this path, there's a cultural context obstructing our way here. The notion of eye contact bespeaks a variety of social do's and don'ts, based on the connotations of physical intimacy. This is another checkpoint on the medicine path for many, a place to become aware of and step over your ego.

The beauty of this exercise is that it's alarmingly simple to do, but it's so rarely done, even with those with whom we are most intimate. There's real power to doing this with someone you're already in a close relationship with (friends, lovers, mothers, fathers), but it's just as incredible to do it with a complete stranger. You'll be surprised at what the experience can bring you. It rarely disappoints.

THE EXERCISE:

This works best when both parties are already de-stressed and fully present, so do whatever you need to do to achieve this state. A 15-minute meditation, yoga routine, breathing exercise, long walk in nature, or your favorite variety of the hot/cold therapy mentioned at the end of Chapter 3 would work well here.

1. Set a timer for 10 minutes.

2. Sit across from your partner, preferably cross-legged on a soft rug or cushion.

3. Close your eyes and take a few deep breaths.

4. Open your eyes and look into the eyes of the person in front of you for 10 minutes.

5. Let the muscles in your face and body respond naturally to whatever is occurring in the gaze. This isn't a staring contest; blinking is allowed.

6. No talking.

After the 10 minutes are up, you can decide whether you want to share your experience with your partner. Sometimes a conversation seems like a natural extension of what you just experienced, and other times it feels right to give a hug, acknowledge each other, and let the encounter be what it is.

Old Buddhist teachings tell us that we're all mirrors for one another, seeing the truth of our inner landscape reflected in the eyes of those around us, but it's easy for this to go in one ear and out the other. After a few eye gazes, these words will mean something entirely different to you.

Chapter 11

◇◇◇◇◇◇◇◇◇◇◇◇◇◇◇◇

BREAKING DOWN TO BREAK THROUGH

There came a time when staying tight within the bud became more painful than the strain it took to bloom.

—ANAÏS NIN

November 12, 2010
Loreto Province, Peru

There are three levels of personal wetness during the rainy season.

The baseline is damp. Every morning you wake with some degree of moisture in your bedding and perspiration in your undergarments. The first few days are an adjustment, but after a week or so it just is.

The next and, in my opinion, *least* desirable of the three tiers of personal humidity is moist. Moist is when you're walking through the jungle with some type of waterproofing layer on, trying hard to remain only damp but failing at it. Half of your senses are clinging to the patches of torso that are still holding out against the encroaching drips down your back while you plod on toward a semidry shelter. Resistance is futile.

Then there's soaked—the point past which surrender to the elements is the only option left to you. Water has overwhelmed your defenses and claimed every inch of your body. The only useful clothing left to you are your knee-high mud boots, which are at least keeping your toes from plunging into whatever might be hidden in the mud underfoot. Oddly enough, once you've flinched and shuddered away the discomfort, soaked is not a terrible place to be.

Soaked is the state of the crew and me as we plod through the forest in the direction of Hut 7 on Day 29.

With only two days left in our healing retreat, we're making rounds to each of the patients to conduct final check-in interviews and document how far they have come.

The day started off sunny, but the skies opened up about two hours ago, and we've been swimming through the bush, doing our best to keep the equipment dry on the sprints between huts.

We just left Hut 4, where Melinda surprised all of us with a very vulnerable and honest summary of where she is in her process right now. I'm no shaman, but the spiritual transformation in her is obvious. She came into this journey as an overly confident natural health maven who had all the answers. The kind of person who tells the doctor what is wrong with her and only occasionally hears the advice she is being given by the professionals she has put her trust in.

When the shamans attempted to dig into the shadows that were looming in the form of self-distraction mechanisms, inner narratives, and an overly dogmatic approach to her spirit path, there would always be a subtle bob and weave on her part. But over the past 10 days, something has shifted, and the 58-year-old mother of two has become silent and introspective. She was a hard nut to crack for the first few weeks, but the jungle has brought her into the embrace we've seen in most of the other patients.

It's hard to say if Melinda's breast cancer has improved or worsened over the past month, though. The herb poultices that

Edwin has been preparing for her haven't had any obvious effect on the growth of the tumor on the right side of her chest.

The shamans were concerned when they discovered she had already had a mastectomy to remove an earlier tumor in the same place. According to them, once the body has been mutilated (their word) or burned using chemotherapy and radiation, it's much harder for the herbs and ceremonies to do their work.

Melinda believes the treatment is working and asks if she can stay on for another 30 days. I tell her that I'll relay her request to Roman and ask him to come out and visit her. The answer is most likely going to be yes.

The muddy path underfoot turns into a stream as the forest floor gives way to a steep downward slope pointing in the direction of Hut 7. John is our final stop.

"Lens on camera one is starting to fog up," Brock, our lead cameraman, says without the urgency that would usually be attached to a gear malfunction of this caliber. The mood today is light and happy despite the torrential downpour we find ourselves in.

After all, we're soaked, not moist. That, and the enlightened state of our fearless patients, has us all in high spirits. Plus, we've got another dry camera with us and only two days to go.

I haven't seen John since the San Pedro ceremony yesterday, which I left in dazzling fashion after nature called on me a second time. Nor have any of the other crew or staff members seen him, aside from Roman.

The storm clouds overhead shed a false dusk on the stretch of forest ahead as we approach Hut 7. There are candles lit inside as we slosh up to the front steps.

"John, are you home?"

"Nick, Dan, Brock! Come inside." The door swings inward, revealing a smiling John. "Please, come inside. You boys are drenched! Talk about dedication to the cause . . ."

John's lighthearted expression beams a three-dimensional luminescence against the dark and stormy jungle just beyond the window behind him.

Dan glances at me from behind camera two with an eyebrow raised slightly off its perch, telepathing "What happened to the old grumpy John, and who the hell is this?"

"John," I begin, "the last time I saw you was in the maloka during San Pedro ceremony. You seemed to be really—"

"Yes," John interjects. "I know. I was shown parts of myself last night that I had long forgotten about. I've been scratching at this thing within me that is always just out of reach. I feel it in my periphery sometimes, a higher part of me that is yearning to be let back in."

He's speaking with a warm smile, but his eyes become teary as he continues.

"I can't even imagine certain aspects of yesterday." He pauses thoughtfully. "You know, it's just beyond comprehension, but I'm aware that it all happened, unfolded, and it was an amazing experience. I mean, my body begins to vibrate as I talk to you about it. You know, real vibration and other 'senseness' of what's here." A huge smile creases his face as tears stream down his cheeks.

He lets out a laugh. "So nothing much is happening for me!"

"How do you feel physically?" I ask. "Do you think you've made any progress with your prostate cancer?"

"I actually haven't thought about that in a few days. Dr. Pretel ran another PSA test a few days ago, and I'm supposed to visit with him one more time before we leave. But after what I've experienced this week, I'd say anything is possible." He is moving around the small hut now, radiating with energy. "I don't think I've felt this young since I was in my 20s. A weight has been lifted off me, Nick, almost as if something toxic or poisonous has been removed from my body. It's like Roman says. Sometimes you have to break down to break through. I feel like the breakdown is complete, and now there are openings inside me where there once were not."

The person before us looks the same as the old John. Same skinny frame, gray eyes, bald cranium with white hair around the sides. But this is a different man. Kind and youthful. Wise.

"Nick, I would like to stay in touch with you once we all return home. I think there are a few things I can share from my humbling experience here in the jungle that might be relevant to you. I've been where you are now, an intrepid explorer in my early 30s who was trying to do good in the world. I respect the path you're on, but there are many traps along the way that I fell into, and I'd like to help you avoid them."

I am a little taken aback at my own role in John's narrative, and my surprise probably shows.

"Anyway," he continues quickly, "let me know if that feels like something you'd be interested in. It was an idea inspired by the cactus medicine last night. After I came back."

A few days ago, this idea honestly wouldn't have held much appeal for me, but the man is speaking truth and transmitting an essence in his demeanor that has us all in awe.

"That would be great, John," I reply sincerely. "I'll take all the help I can get. Thank you."

In two days, John will have his final checkup with Dr. Pretel, who will give him some stunning news about his most recent PSA test. PSA stands for prostate-specific antigen, and the test is a standard measure used in modern medicine to screen for prostate cancer in men, usually over the age of 40. My father was diagnosed with prostate cancer using this method, and although it's not 100 percent accurate, it's helped thousands if not millions of men detect this condition before it's too late.

When John arrived, his PSA levels were above 7.5, and his doctor had already diagnosed his prostate cancer using a biopsy. On the final day of the retreat, Dr. Pretel will perform another PSA test, and the new results will show that he's dropped to 5.5. Although it's only 2 points lower, this is a sweeping shift on this particular test. A 5.5 PSA level is considered to be normal for men John's age, and his doctors back in Australia will be shocked when they get the results.

He is one of five patients who experience a breakthrough with their illnesses on this trip. This statistic will become a catchy tagline for *The Sacred Science* documentary's film festival run—"Five patients will return healed. Two will return disappointed. And one won't come back at all." Cue suspenseful music.

ADMIT ONE (YOUR FREE TICKET TO WATCH THE *SACRED SCIENCE* DOCUMENTARY)

In the middle of an ayahuasca ceremony a few years ago, I was "shown" quite bluntly by a higher power that the *Sacred Science* movie needed to be given away *for free* so that people of all walks of life, regardless of socioeconomic status, could witness the healing truths of these ancient traditions.

We have since made the *Sacred Science* film available for anyone in the world to watch online, at no cost. That includes you, dear reader.

To date, the documentary has been viewed by more than two million people and has birthed its own tribe of conscious-minded individuals.

If you would like to witness the transformative journey of our eight patients, find out what happened to each of them, and learn more about the herbs that were used for their specific illnesses, please use the Internet link below. There are no strings attached—you can watch it and share it with whomever you wish.

Here is the link to use: http://thesacredscience.com/tssbook_moviescreening.

Although the physical results of our patients are promising, they're not evenly distributed across the group. Some of these daring participants have experienced borderline miraculous recoveries from serious illnesses, while others are still struggling with their symptoms.

But one extremely positive outcome has been reported by everyone. This past month has given each patient a cathartic spiritual opening, more powerful than anything else they have experienced in their lives. Even those who are "disappointed" with their physical recovery thus far are seeing themselves and the world around them with new eyes.

Many are reporting daily experiences of synchronicity and coincidence. The crew has been overwhelmed by it as well, to the point where it is no longer even spoken about. Unexplainable phenomena have become the new normal.

John's breakthrough is not entirely unique. Other patients speak of similar realizations. *Why haven't I let others in? Why haven't I been there for the people who are most important to me? Why these walls of separation?*

But John's description of feeling the need to be a lone wolf rather than part of the pack sticks with me. We Westerners have forgotten what it means to be part of a pack and to let that pack take care of us.

Of the startling transformations that have transpired in our monthlong healing retreat, this one transmission will be my own personal catalyst. Science hasn't figured out how to measure or prove it yet, but we humans are more connected than we think we are. We've somehow gone down a road of separation from our loved ones, our neighbors, and ultimately ourselves, and it's time to come back to our true nature.

But we all have shadows we must first be willing to face.

■ ■ ■

The following evening, every resident of the center is invited to a closing fire ceremony in a jungle clearing next to the maloka. Dan and I fiddle with a camera next to a towering pile of dried wood while patients, shamans, and staff situate themselves on random chairs and strategically placed logs.

The feeling of this rare informal gathering is lighthearted and bittersweet. The patients have come such a long way, and this is the first and only opportunity they will have to share their experiences and express their gratitude before beginning the long voyage home in the morning.

Gretchen, whose debilitating IBS is now completely healed, smiles as she tells Nicola about her son, Aiden, whom she misses immensely and cannot wait to see upon returning to Wisconsin.

Jessica, still in the throes of her Crohn's disease symptoms, is explaining to John how she will be staying at the center for an extra month to continue working with the plants. He praises her for her bravery and takes down her information, promising to check in from Australia now and again.

Juan is busy helping Edwin and Christian lay a few more branches on the eight-foot-high pyramid of wood, listening intently to some instruction Edwin is giving him. He came here struggling with depression and substance abuse issues but is an entirely different person right now. Not only are Juan's symptoms entirely gone, but he has realized his true calling: to be a healer. Over the past week, the shamans have made a special exception to the rules, allowing him to accompany them on their rounds each morning as they prepared herbal treatments and attended to the other patients. Last night we visited Juan in his hut and he opened up about his time here.

"It's the most significant thing I've ever done," he told us, "learning how to be at peace with myself here in the wilderness and keep moving forward through the pain and fear.

"I realize now that the issues we all have are not physical. We feel them physically; the disease comes out and we often experience it in a three-dimensional sense. But I see now that it really comes from here [pointing to his head] and here [pointing to his heart], right? We create these things, and if you deal with them in here, then the physical symptoms will go away. That's what the shamans work with—that's what's going on in the jungle."

The sun has fully set and the conversations are illuminated by headlamps expertly pointed at the ground by each wearer to provide ambient lighting. The sea of stars above us shines brilliantly in the cosmos, a side benefit of being more than 500 miles from the nearest city.

Edwin and Christian are pouring some kind of liquid on and around the base of the stack of timber as Roman steps forward and begins to speak.

"This is our final night together, here under the Amazon sky. The past month has been both challenging and enlightening for you all, but the true work has only begun. Everything you have learned about yourselves, every layer of illusion that you have peeled away, *every healing you have experienced* is only as permanent as your daily practice allows it to be.

"When you return to the lives from which you came, the clarity you now have will be tested. This is not a possibility; this is a fact. The question is, can you walk through this world and hold on to what you have been shown?

"People with the experience of thousands of years have seen that each level of our personal evolution comes with its own pitfalls. The sacred science—the shamanic system of healing that you are immersed in right now—was brought forth from these native traditions as a beacon of light to guide us through the ocean of our subconscious, so we don't get lost and forget who we truly are.

"You have seen each other laid bare in the face of the unknown and now know what is possible when we embrace the deeper parts of ourselves. You each have your own spirit path to walk, but it is our shared duty to stay awake and fully present with everything we encounter in our lives from here forward."

Edwin approaches with a flaming branch and hands it to Roman. *"Listo, hermano."* Roman takes the makeshift torch and turns back to us.

"This assemblage of dried wood behind me symbolizes all those things within yourself that you have let go of this past month. All of the non-serving thoughts, the tall tales you have been repeating to yourselves about who you are, the traumatic memories of your past, the string of words and thoughts that were quietly imprisoning you . . ."

The shaman approaches the pile and touches the flaming branch to the outermost cuttings, igniting small patches of petroleum. The fire travels quickly to the center of the temporary structure, licking hungrily at each log, leaf, and twig as it goes.

"This flame is a symbol of the light of consciousness we all possess. It can transform the darkness within and without us into understanding and truth. The shadows we harbor are just waiting to be illuminated by this essential state of being, but we must be willing to hold the torch and explore every aspect of ourselves with an open heart."

The fire grows taller and hotter behind Roman, reaching 15 feet upward into the sky. Crackling embers shoot out from the top and then float, dancing against the sparkling stars above.

We sit in silence, transfixed by the burning form that is fast disappearing into nothingness. Looking around the circle, I see a collection of the bravest souls I've ever met.

FACING OUR SHADOWS

Consider them both, the sea and the land; and do you not find a strange analogy to something in yourself? For as this appalling ocean surrounds the verdant land, so in the soul of man there lies one insular Tahiti, full of peace and joy, but encompassed by all the horrors of the half-known life.

—HERMAN MELVILLE, *MOBY-DICK*

One evening in the middle of a coca ceremony with Roman, I came to a sudden realization and found myself speaking it aloud.

"I have an anger inside me that I don't know what to do with," I began. "But I have a convenient victim complex that justifies the shadow. It tells me, 'Yeah, maybe you have anger, but you needed it to get through life when you were younger. You had to learn to be tough and protect yourself.'"

I looked across the tight alcove at the cross-legged shaman, who sat against the wall opposite me, and something in his face prompted me to continue. "There's a built-in justification in the way I tell it. When I open up about this hot anger that I sometimes feel, I always lead with the fact that I was bullied when I was younger."

"Tell me about this bullying," he said at last. "How old were you?"

Everyone enters this spirit path with their own set of skeletons in the closet that need to be removed in order to continue forward. Many of mine stem from unresolved strands of "outcast consciousness" from my childhood.

When I was young, the simple act of going to school carried an extreme amount of anxiety. I never understood why, but I didn't have any friends from kindergarten through high school. Maybe it's because I had a stutter, or maybe I stuttered because I didn't have any friends—either way, I was alone. I wasn't even "nerd" or "geek" status, I was an island unto myself in an ocean of kids who seemed to be thriving in their elementary and middle school environment.

I could never figure out the friend game that everyone else was playing so well. My mom always used to tell me not to worry, that we Polizzi boys were late bloomers and that it would get easier as I got older. It didn't for more than 10 years.

At lunch, most kids have a select group of friends they find in the cafeteria and flock to like clockwork each day. That wasn't how it was for me. I remember the hot panic that would come over me as I loaded my lunch tray with whatever overly processed, prison-grade gruel they gave us back then, all the while peering around the lunchroom looking for a safe place to sit down.

A safe place could be identified as a table occupied by mild-mannered boys who wouldn't balk at my joining them— these were ideal. The less-great option would be to find an empty table and sit alone, but that would often prompt taunting from kids at other tables who astutely pointed out that I didn't have any friends. Sometimes I just skipped lunch altogether.

I had sweaty hands throughout my entire childhood. My notebooks and test papers were covered in cloudy black smudges where the side of my wet hand brushed across fresh ink or pencil lead. My fingers were almost constantly clenched into nervous fists, my jaw set tight. I can still envision the shiny micro-rivers of sweat that flowed through the creases in my palms nonstop.

Things escalated in eighth grade, and there was some physical confrontation with a few different kids at recess. This is when I found out that I had a rage inside me. I was too embarrassed to maneuver inside the lunchroom, but when someone was trying to physically force me into submission, something inside me would snap. Onlooking boys called it "retard strength."

Whatever it was, this reaction was an ally that got me through some tough situations.

In college and my early 20s, the rage came in handy when I felt that friends were being harassed at bars or that girls were being disrespected. My wife, Michelle, even thinks it's kind of sexy.

It still lives inside me, decades after my fighting days ended. After all the inner work I've done on this path, this self-defense mechanism still remains and is one of the core wounds that I am in the process of healing right now.

"This is a blessing in disguise," Roman offered gently. "It's a matter of taking responsibility and recognizing your power. The basic ignorance that I'm seeing behind the story you just shared is that you're bullying yourself, giving your power away, developing this conditioning of hardening rather than softening. The true strength is not in being defensive, keeping people out, being afraid of being taken advantage of, having this tough and strong attitude. The true strength is in remaining soft and vulnerable, having your heart open in all situations.

"Long ago," he continued, "there lived a Tibetan saint named Milarepa, who also experienced much violence in his early life and was brave enough to face his shadows and work through each one until they were fully dissolved. To do so, he needed to learn to hold space for the darkness that had transpired in his life to such a degree that the greatest light was ultimately born from it."

Roman then shared a prayer about Milarepa, which I will now share with you.

LET YOUR MIND STAY

I can contemplate the sky

But clouds make me uneasy

Milarepa tells me how to meditate on clouds

If the sky's as easy as you say

Clouds are just the sky's play

Let your mind stay within the sky

I can contemplate the sea

But waves make me uneasy

Milarepa tells me how to meditate on waves

If the sea's as easy as you say

Waves are just the sea's play

Let your mind stay within the sea

I can contemplate my mind

But thoughts make me uneasy

Milarepa tells me how to meditate on thoughts

If the mind's as easy as you say

Thoughts are just the mind's play

Let your mind stay within your mind

Shadow work is learning how to be free from fear and emotional blocks, not by avoidance but by understanding them. By developing recognition of who you are and learning how to become a channel or a hollow bone, you realize that whatever you are feeling is just the clouds moving through the sky. They may be dark clouds, but if my true nature is the sky, I don't need to identify with the anger. It's moving through me.

If you are completely open to any thoughts and sensations that are coming through you, then gradually you can recognize yourself as that pure, indestructible state of consciousness that cannot be affected or bound by anything. That's what fearlessness is. You know who you are, you know what your nature is, and no matter what goes through you or happens around you, it cannot affect your true, essential state.

This is part of doing shadow work: staying present and learning how to maintain restful, heart-centered presence, period.

There are a number of practices that can help one work through fears and shadows, but meditation and a consciously lived life are the best teachers.

Chapter 12

◇◇◇◇◇◇◇◇◇◇◇◇◇◇

WIRED FOR TRIBE

June 19, 2016, 5:00 A.M.
Larapata, Peru

The sun is cresting the eastern wall of the Mapacho Valley as I wander through the morning mist along a footpath above the Paititi base camp. I can't sleep late when I'm in a tent, and this morning the inconvenience is an absolute gift. My eyes are fixed on a few locals ascending an adjacent coca field with heavy bags on their backs. They move quickly, as if the 45-degree incline underfoot does not exist. How?

A rooster crows somewhere down below.

It's almost time to get down to breakfast, but I don't want to leave this spot. I stare up and realize I'm standing next to a huge *vilca* tree, the great-grandfather spirit of the jungle.

Condor medicine.

The Incan shamans used the seeds of this *Anadenanthera colubrina* tree in a sacred snuff that would help them transcend this world and enter the realm of the spirits. When the right dose is sniffed, the effects are extreme, starting with terrible pain in the head and then turning into what many consider to be an evil or dark realm of consciousness where death seems to be close at hand. This shadow state lingers for 10 to 20 minutes, finally giving way to something much more euphoric and light.

Each of the major plant teachers in this tradition have a corresponding animal spirit; Grandmother Ayahuasca is often depicted as a serpent or snake, Grandfather San Pedro (or Huachuma) is connected to the puma, and Great Grandfather Vilca is represented by the condor. Each of these creatures give us insight into the action the sacred medicine has once it enters our body and the abilities it unlocks. Vilca is thought by many to be the ultimate plant teacher, often delivering those who are brave enough to partake into the heavens and then back again.

A transmission runs down my spine. This tree relies on all its branches, leaves, and roots to interface with the outside environment in a harmonious way in order to survive and thrive. There is no one part that is more important than the others; there is no separation among its many constituents. Every inch of this vilca has an important role to play, and the health of the surrounding jungle depends on each tree like this one living in full connection with its neighbors.

We're not much different from trees in this respect. The system of life-flow that is so essential to a healthy forest also applies to the two-legged mammals that walk the trails carved into its soil. It can be summed up in one word: *tribe.*

To many, this word feels exotic or of a different cultural ilk, but I think it's time we begin to bring the true meaning of tribe back into our modern lives.

In today's world, our connection via the interweb does loosely match tribe's definition: a group of people linked by social, economic, religious, or blood ties. But for the traditional people of the world, tribe takes place in much closer proximity. It's the extended family, the community in which each member shares and cares for the others.

In tribal societies, everything is shared: successes, failures, responsibilities, leadership. No single life occurrence is too intense or overwhelming for an individual to handle, because he or she doesn't need to shoulder the burden alone.

For the Dagura tribe of Burkina Faso, for example, when a death occurs, the entire village joins together in a complex and beautiful grief ritual that lasts for several days. Support for mourners continues long after the death, as grief is seen as a community event.

In tribal societies, success is also shared. No success is so large that a person's ego explodes, because accomplishments are the result of a group endeavor.

For the Enawene Nawe tribe of Brazil, the Yãkwa ritual is a time for the tribe to spend several months fishing along the Amazon River by canoe, smoking the fish as they go, finally returning to their villages with sustenance to last for months. Everyone wins, everyone celebrates, everyone is nourished.

Here in the United States, our sense of tribe has largely vanished. Many ship their elders off to isolated retirement communities. We work our lives away so we can afford our private houses, our individual cars, our gizmos and gadgets that keep us disconnected from each other.

Meanwhile, our children are growing up without the wisdom of their grandparents. Kids are left to their own devices, and these days those devices have screens. Many young people have swapped personal connection for an electronic interface.

For an organism to function, all of its parts must be intact. If we look at our society as an organism, with the nuclear family at its core, all signs point to an organism that is disjointed and blocked.

No one wants to feel like their lives lack meaning, like many of our retirees do. When tribal folks enter their later years, they make the natural transition from provider to wisdom-keeper. It is their time to emerge as teachers, caregivers for children, and a grounding force for young adults and parents. Their role shifts, but they are just as needed.

Children of the tribe have two or three generations of role models, each with their own unique life perspective to bestow.

As a parent, I see how important my son River's relationship with his grandparents is. They teach him a way of being that I simply don't have access to yet. It's magical and profoundly fulfilling to watch them interact.

This is just a glimpse of what is possible when we humans live in a fully interconnected way. So many of us feel alone and overwhelmed in our lives, even though we have loving friends and family. Could it be that we need community in order to share this human experience in a more meaningful way?

I believe that "tribe" is the prescription for many of the pitfalls in the modern world. But to obtain this antidote, we must learn how to be in relationship with one another again—with our families, with our neighbors, and spreading outward from there.

Over and over nowadays, I hear the same message: our needs and the needs of our loved ones are not being met. The irony is that our needs are all connected. The need of grandparents to have meaning can be fulfilled by bringing them closer to the family and their grandchildren. The need of parents to have support and some time for themselves can be accomplished by the same act. Our children's need for human connection, attention, and mentorship can also be filled by bringing back the tribe.

There are so many inefficiencies in the way we've set ourselves up. They just don't make sense. If we are open to their wisdom, the indigenous tribes of the planet and the forest itself have a lot to teach us.

■   ■   ■

Dogs in Peru and the rest of Latin America are wild creatures, mostly left to their own devices. If you've traveled through Mexico and the countries that unfurl as you navigate southward, you've probably had some encounters with street dogs. They're a little nippy, usually cross-bred, and often in need of several baths. But they have an unusual intelligence not seen in most cul-de-sac dogs in the States, and although their mutt pedigree would keep them light-years away from "best in show," they are beautiful and resilient animals.

These pups all seem as friendly and innocuous as domesticated pets, but it's clear that in fact they have no owners. You see them lying around on the cobble streets in the morning, soaking up the sun, then wandering over to the cooler stone threshold of a shady doorway during the hotter hours. In the morning and at dusk, you'll see them roaming solo or in packs, on the prowl for food, mating partners, and a little adventure. Yes, they're mangy and flea ridden, but they sure seem content with their lot in life.

A few months ago, I was at a wedding in a pocket canyon in the Sacred Valley, about three kilometers (almost two miles) up the mountain from the small Peruvian town of Lamay, when I spotted a mutt wandering through a bull pasture. My friend Marc and I immediately recognized her from a trek we had taken a few months prior, about 20 miles north of where we were standing.

Quiet but joyful, this brown and scrawny lab mix loped over to us and lay down at my feet, resting her head gently on my left boot. Within a minute she was sound asleep. I was amazed and grateful to see her again, and somewhat shocked that she could have found her way so casually through these harsh mountains. What is the range of a South American street dog?

It's not unusual for a gray wolf to travel up to 20 or 30 miles in the course of a day, but we don't tend to ponder the roaming radius of a domesticated—or semidomesticated—canine.

Maybe the magic of these Andean strays is that they're a combination of domesticated and wild, able to abide by the rules of a human home but also tough enough to survive in the outside world for weeks and months at a time.

By contrast, I have a purebred French bulldog named Oscar back at home who is loving, playful, always hungry, perpetually farting, and a champion snorer. We love him to death, but he wouldn't last an hour on the streets, let alone in more rugged terrain.

When Michelle and I first moved in together in New York City about eight years ago, she insisted that we get a dog—and specifically, a purebred French bulldog. She wasn't 100 percent sold on me as her permanent life partner yet, so even though I was not a firm believer in the majesty of mutts at that point, saying no to her was not in the cards. My only condition was that I got to pick out the dog.

One rainy afternoon, we took the Q train out to a breeder in Sheepshead Bay who had advertised a few pups for sale on Craigslist. The adorable pictures and official logo on the web page looked pretty legit, but we found ourselves standing outside a run-down walkup under a subway overpass, ringing the bell beside a beat-up black door with the house number scrawled across it in what looked like white chalk.

The man who answered the door was nice enough and led us upstairs to the second floor, which was brightly lit with freshly painted white walls, some official-looking signage, and a make-shift front desk. He asked us to sit down on a nearby IKEA couch while he went and got the puppies. I scowled at Michelle and said something about this being a bad idea; then the breeder returned with two tiny handfuls of fur and wrinkles. He set the two-month-old puppies on the floor in front of us, and any semblance of grouchiness or concern I might have harbored about getting a purebred dog evaporated instantly.

The burrito-size fuzz brothers were so tiny and innocent, but they already had their own character and disposition. One was more cavalier, padding over to a basket of dog toys and jump-ing into it with reckless abandon. The other just sat there staring at us with big eyes, sizing us up. The pup in the basket was yip-ping and yapping away, but this one didn't make a sound. He just watched us.

His brother got bored with the toy he was chewing on in the corner and turned his sights on us. Springing into action, he ran full tilt and barreled into the pup in front of us. But the calmer one reacted in a split second, rolling with his brother's momen-tum until he was on top, pinning the ball of fur and teeth to the floor almost effortlessly.

A moment later he was back over at our feet, studying us, occa-sionally licking his paw while he glanced over at the disinterested breeder at his desk.

"We'll take this one," I said, affirming the choice that had already been made by the puppy at our feet.

And that was how Oscar came into our lives. He was only supposed to grow to 25 pounds or so, but he now hangs out around the 40-pound mark, give or take a meal or two. He used to be the most athletic French bulldog I had ever seen, able to chase down Frisbees in midair and sometimes beat more conventionally agile dogs in short sprints at the park.

Until he reached the ripe old age of six.

While playing with another dog one day, Oscar took a short tumble down some steps and knocked one of his vertebrae out of alignment. This type of fall wouldn't have affected most other dogs, but we soon found out that French bulldogs are known to have misshapen spines caused by extreme overbreeding. The average life span of a Frenchie is 10 years if it's lucky, but those later years are often quite a struggle.

Through centuries of husbandry, these creatures have been carefully mutated into their present form, with attributes that please us aesthetically but leave them hamstrung in terms of basic survival. Their bodies are now so out of whack that they can't even reproduce without human assistance.

It's hard to believe that Oscar and all domesticated dogs are direct descendants of *Canis lupus*, the gray wolf. Dog is man's best friend, but maybe he's also a mirror, reflecting in full detail how we've bred them—and ourselves—away from our innate, primordial origins.

Drawing comparisons between dogs and people or puppies and children is not a very popular thing to do at cocktail parties, but this book isn't politically correct, nor ought it be. I'm looking for truth rather than accepted fact, and some of our cultural norms must be put aside to get there.

We've domesticated the dickens out of our dogs and cats, and whether we'd like to admit it or not, we've done the same to ourselves. What is at the core of this way of thinking?

Control. Predictability. Possession. Domination.

These four words are cousins to a four-letter word that begins with *F*. It's something that we must come to terms with and constantly overcome on the spirit path: *fear*.

In many cases fear is healthy, if not vitally important. Without it, I would almost certainly have perished by now, and the same goes for you, whether you acknowledge it or not. Fear is our friend, as long as the frequency and dose are right. Looking at the prevailing news headlines and the decrease in social behaviors that indicate trust in strangers—like hitchhiking, for instance—I would say as a society we are overdosing on it.

Like Oscar, we are all bred and trained to live within a cultural and technological context. This has its perks, especially when you're taken out of the food chain as a young pup, but what would Oscar do if we left him outside to fend for himself? He'd die within a few days unless he found another household to take him in and put food in his bowl.

What would happen if technology as we know it failed? If the entire power grid of the East or West Coast were knocked out and electricity, Internet, and cell phones were shut off, what would the fallout be?

How many of us would survive? Would you?

I can almost guarantee you the indigenous folks of South America would. And don't think they're technologically inferior, because they have cell phones and computer access too. They simply haven't forgotten what it's like to be a human being in a natural environment.

Raised to trust their instincts, to learn from direct experience with the outer world, and to be tough, Amazonian and Andean folk aren't dependent on much besides Mother Nature herself for survival. They are sharp, filled with grit, and, perhaps most important, contagiously happy with comparatively little.

This disconnection from our natural environment shows itself in other ways too. We suffer from back problems caused by sitting for hours each day and eye problems from a lifetime under fluorescent lights, staring at computer screens and televisions, passing our time watching actors portray fictitious events and newscasters blast our brains with overly sensationalized, fear-based renditions of world events.

There is a void inside us that no amount of network television, binge-watched sitcoms, or video games will ever fill. Something primordial is crying out for deeper connection to others and to the ground beneath our feet.

Did you know that our not-too-distant ancestors briskly walked more than two miles a day on average? We come from hunter-gatherer societies whose survival depended on working seamlessly together, and our physiology and psychology are still very much oriented toward that lifestyle. Heroics, shared burdens, and faith in the collective were daily realities for our ancestors— but where are they now?

Technology seems to have eclipsed the speed of our biological evolution.

If this technology were done away with, whether voluntarily or by some cataclysmic event, would we hominids naturally gravitate toward our innate tendencies, or are we too far removed from the natural world and one another to come together and thrive?

DISSOLVING THE ILLUSION OF SEPARATION

Have you ever been to a nude beach or a "clothing optional" hot spring? Odd question, I know, but I promise this is going somewhere. There's a very interesting phenomenon that occurs when we remove our clothes in a crowd of other naked humans. The childishness of societal norms around clothing becomes almost immediately obvious.

Before stripping down to your birthday suit, there may be some trepidation, fear of judgment, anxiety about inviting unwanted attention, and so on. But when everyone is naked, we're all in the same boat. Slightly more vulnerable, but also more free. You might think there would be kinkiness involved in a mass of naked people in a hot spring, but it's actually an extremely normal and nonsexual affair. If you've done it, you know what I'm talking about. If you haven't, I encourage you to give it a try.

In many ways, the idea of sharing one's inner work with others presents similar vulnerability and opportunity for freedom. It's a little scary at first, but once everyone has their cards on the table, we get the immensely therapeutic reminder that we're all human, and we're all perfectly flawed. Once we know what the other is working on, that relationship becomes much richer and far easier to navigate. Your loved ones become mirrors for you, empowered to provide insights that might bring you closer to your medicine as well.

Perhaps most important, openly communicating with trusted friends about what you're working on to improve yourself will encourage them to pursue their own work, allowing them to heal by association with the path you're on. As we walk down this path, it becomes very clear that we're all mirrors for one another, reflecting a unified consciousness, separated only by the flesh and bone of these vessels we inhabit—and maybe not even.

Syncing up with one another and becoming clear channels of the essence might seem a bit creepy. It might even sound . . . communist? I know it did for me at first. Until the part where it became contagiously liberating.

The eye-gazing exercise mentioned in Chapter 10 is a great way to dissolve separation one-on-one, but here's an exercise you can do in a group of three or more.

SHADOW SHOW-AND-TELL

How often do you find yourself having the same old conversation at a dinner with old friends or family members? You talk about work, the kids if you have any, some scandalous gossip about mutual friends, and then the old trip down memory lane. Remember the time?

These surface dialogues are rote and mind-numbingly detached of any real vulnerability or evolutionary assistance. Aren't these the humans whom you consider to be among your most trusted associates? It's time to lay your cards on the table and invite them to do the same.

Next time you're sitting across from a member of your inner circle, offer something that you've been struggling with on an emotional, behavioral, or spiritual level. This will most likely draw some feedback and, one hopes, empathy. The seed of group transformation has now been planted.

Regardless of how your kindred comrades respond, listen with full presence to what they say for a few minutes. Then, when you have an opportunity, lay down some game rules to keep it interesting.

Say something like this: "Everyone, I am totally cool with discussing this further, and I am ready to really hear your insights on what I'm working on. But in order for this to feel like a level playing field, I think we should all share something we're going through right now and need help with. Easy admissions don't count."

If you shared something truly personal to start with, you've now set the bar for what is to come next. Your friends will either agree to play or they won't. But either one of those responses will give you some good information about who your people are. Most likely, you will find that your transparency with your own struggle opens the door and creates a safe space for your friends to do the same.

Your group has now entered an entirely new level of relationship. You look at them differently when you interact and are able to recognize their struggles in real time and hold space for that.

This is a way to see through perceived separation and begin a tribe.

A word of warning, though: Dissolving the veil of separation requires us to see beyond the conditioning and stale thought constructs that are prevalent in much of the modern, private property–obsessed world. Expect to suffer and struggle a little at first. It's a necessary part of growth.

If you find it deeply unsettling to share who you are with others, this in itself is a prime target for deeper exploration and ultimately—drumroll, please—*the work.*

Chapter 13

◇◇◇◇◇◇◇◇◇◇◇◇◇

ASCENT

*As dreams are the healing songs from the wilderness of our
unconscious—so wild animals, wild plants, wild landscapes are
the healing dreams from the deep singing mind of the earth.*

—Dale Pendell

June 19, 2016, 8:00 A.M.
Larapata, Peru

I t's been six years since we filmed *The Sacred Science*, but it feels
like six months.

Today is ceremony day, and we'll all be convening at the
chapel tonight at 9 P.M. to drink ayahuasca and hold space for anything that arises during the eight-hour ritual.

I figured we would take it easy today and shake off the sore-
ness from our heroic trek down the mountain last night, but it
appears Roman has other plans. I find Elton and Roman in the
dining hall eating the Amazonian ayahuasca breakfast—a bowl of
unseasoned quinoa and boiled green plantains—and sit down to
join them.

"I want to show you and Mileen our permaculture farm today,
and maybe we can stop by the new school we're helping to build

for the local children as well." Roman actually appears to be enjoying the bowl of flavorless mush in front of him as he speaks through mouthfuls.

"Sounds great," I say. "Is it close to here?"

Elton looks at me and chuckles, pointing his finger toward the valley wall that looms above us. "See the top of that ridge? There's another ridge beyond that one. That's where we're going. Eat up, brother. We're going to have a hike today."

The Paititi Institute sits on 1,000 hectares (about 2,500 acres) of high jungle, about a five-hour drive and then a two-hour hike east of the Sacred Valley and the nearest city, Cusco. The base camp, where everyone eats, sleeps, and showers, is situated at the bottom of the valley, a few hundred feet above the fast waters of the Mapacho River, which provides a constant background rumble to all daily and nightly activities.

From the eco village on the riverbank, the land sprawls upward at an extreme pitch, hiding within it ancient Incan terraces, patchworks of old-growth forest, craggy rock faces, and mysterious waterfalls. What they all call "the Land" is essentially the western half of a small mountain, nestled along the easternmost reaches of the Andes Mountains, where alpine meets jungle.

The four of us gather outside the dining hall and load our packs with some light gear and water for the trek. The trail above us zigzags upward at what appears to be a 45-degree angle. The next few hours are going to be brutal.

"One step at a time, brother." Roman says as he dons an old, wide-brimmed fedora.

About 30 minutes into our ascent, Roman stops and smiles back at me. "Check this out." Just ahead, the narrow trail bends around a fold in the mountain and out of sight. We round the turn and the hot afternoon air abruptly cools. The forest darkens as we walk deeper into the crease. The dry crunch of boots on hardscrabble is drowned out by the splash of water on rock.

A thin stream is shooting out of a huge rock about 50 feet above us and pounding into a small pool at our feet. "There are many of these sacred places on this land," Roman says. "This water is spring fed and can be drunk—as long as an animal hasn't died in the stream above us." He laughs as he steps closer to the waterfall and catches some of the falling liquid in cupped hands, then brings it up to his lips. "Nothing like it. Try some."

My self-preservation instincts tell me no, but I'm thirsty. It's been more than six years and the shaman hasn't killed me yet. I take my leather gaucho hat off and use it to catch some of the sparkling stuff. The first hatful goes over my head, and with just a split second of hesitation, I pour the second one in the direction of my mouth. He's right—it's actually sweet with maybe a tinge of earthiness.

"*Hermano*, how much farther until we get to the farm?"

Roman looks across the pool at Elton, who replies matter-of-factly, "We're about a quarter of the way there, maybe less."

The four of us are already drenched in sweat from the short but steep climb from the center to where we now stand. Mileen smiles at me, always lighthearted even in challenging circumstances. "I'm glad I've been doing my Pilates lately," he tells me. "The combination of the altitude, heat, and 90-degree vertical is a hell of a workout."

Roman sits on a moist, mossy rock wall, unconcerned by the wetness. "You two haven't sat in ceremony in a while. We are going to work your physical bodies hard today on these trails so they don't get in your way tonight. Don't worry; your muscles will get the rest they need in the chapel while your spirit does the walking."

We ascend another few thousand feet in the next two hours, stepping through three different climate zones as we go—from high jungle to altiplano up to the beginning of a more alpine region—seeing the vegetation and soil change every 20 or 30 minutes. Just putting one boot in front of the other on these Incan trails has become a rite in itself.

As we haul ourselves upward toward the highly anticipated permaculture farm above, I find myself grateful for the discomfort, the burning in knees and calves, the labored breaths. Usually the day of a ceremony is tough for me, each hour filled with quiet dread about what is going to transpire that evening. Some of the veterans absolutely love Grandma, looking forward to each ceremony for weeks in advance.

Not me.

She has shown me more than any other spiritual intervention I've encountered, but her guidance comes at a price. To work with this ancient plant medicine, you have to be willing to look at everything that's hiding in the crevices of your subconscious mind. At least that's how it is for me.

Sometimes it's so intense that I can hardly breathe. I've lost my way before, not knowing who, what, or where I was for hours at a time. But after the reacquaintance with your unmeasurable, unnamable soul-self, the teachings come—sometimes out of the abyss in a very nonlinear manner and sometimes from the voice of Grandma herself. It takes a small death to get there, but it's the most powerful medicine I know. The Quechua word *aya* means soul or death, and *huasca* means vine or rope. *Ayahuasca* literally means vine of the soul.

I've been anxiously anticipating this welcome back ceremony for the past four days, but all this strenuous physical activity is helping my mind relax a little. Roman has proved his wisdom once again. The bodily suffering of scaling these harsh valley walls is dissolving or delaying the pangs of fear that keep trying to creep into my heart. *Thank you, mountain.*

We've now climbed almost the same distance we hiked down last night and can faintly see the road we drove in on, carved into the side of a far-off ridge on the other side of the jungle valley. Hiking up this side is just as steep, but the slow pace makes for a much more controlled and safe journey.

The four of us stop momentarily for a sip of water on an outcropping of rock that provides a commanding view of the Mapacho River below us. The base camp is now just a sprinkle of ant-size rooftops along the thin line of sparkly blue that carves its way along the valley floor.

At about 2 P.M. we reach a simple gate made of hand-hewn wood, with a colorful sign that reads "Bienvenidos." The air has become dry and dusty, definitely a different microclimate up here. Roman lifts the makeshift wire latch, and the old wooden portal creaks, swinging inward on its own weight, inviting us to continue up the trail that lies beyond.

We climb up a steep incline, around yet another switchback. I'm eyeballing the ridgeline above us for some sign of our final destination, when out of nowhere, the craggy path in front of us flattens out into a soft green bed of lush grass. The hard stone and dust underfoot gives way to brown dirt as we slow down and begin to take in our surroundings.

"We're here," Roman announces. He continues walking ahead, past an old well crafted using the same rock construction as the ancient terraces we've been traversing on our ascent. Next to this structure grow two beautiful cacti that I immediately recognize as San Pedro, the Grandfather medicine of the Inca.

The trail ahead forks around a fertile bed of vegetables and then divides again and again, creating a geometric patchwork of colorful crops. Behind this thriving mountain garden is an archaic stone retaining wall, overgrown with moss and rambling vines but still holding strong.

Then it occurs to me. We're standing on one of the many huge terraces that line these mountains, just like the ones we've climbed to get here. The only difference is that this shelf has been restored and is being used as it was originally intended, teeming with fertility and in full production. The Paititi team has taken what already existed and reinvigorated it using a combination of traditional Quechua farming methods and modern permaculture techniques. And it's working.

As we continue on, we come upon a man who is crouched over a bed of collard greens, expertly harvesting ripe leaves and tossing them into a sack over his shoulder. Shirtless and sweaty, he grins up at us from underneath his weather-worn Stetson hat.

"Took you guys long enough! Did you bring me lunch?"

It's Anthony, one of the three apprentices we met last night, and he looks to be completely at home up here. According to Roman, Anthony was drawn to this place by a higher calling; he is here to use his skills to help revitalize these ancient traditions while also learning from a culture that lives in total harmony with nature. In his former life, Anthony was a trail cutter for the United States Forest Service, spending most of his days alone in the wilderness, repairing routes and creating new ones through the American outback.

"Don't worry," Roman says. "We brought you enough quinoa and plantains to feed a village. But let's take these guys up to the cistern and have lunch there."

The word *lunch* triggers an involuntary pang of excitement in my hungry belly that is quickly doused when I think about that quinoa mush and those smeary green plantains. The one positive aspect of this dieta is that it gets our bodies started on the road to discomfort—a primer for the intense sensations to come. My digestive tract is so accustomed to salt and grease that getting the pasty plantains down can be a challenge—the epitome of a first-world problem.

We climb yet another ridge and find ourselves on a high alpine shelf, staring out across a vast network of ridges, peaks, and valleys as far as the eye can see. To our left, the mountains surge upward into the clouds, gradually tapering downward and losing altitude as they drop into the lusher Amazon highlands on our right.

Two dogs have been leading the way since we left the base camp, leaping in and out of view as they follow their ears and noses toward invisible items of interest in the surrounding underbrush. One of them darts across and down a sheer incline on the edge of the path without thinking twice, and I find myself blurting out an involuntary "No!" before I catch myself. These aren't American domesticated dogs. They know what they're doing.

A few minutes later we approach an old stone building with the usual corrugated-metal roof lashed to the top. A sea of golden corncobs is visible from the doorless front entryway. Elton enters first, diving from the threshold into a huge pile of Incan maize. "Gentlemen, this is the year's harvest. Pretty beautiful, huh?" The former chef is in a state of reverence, swimming in sustenance.

Roman wades over to one of two hammocks strung above the two-week-old pile of grain. I make my way toward the other. Body exhausted and leg muscles burning, I plop down and just about fall out of the thing.

"These trails wind all through the Andes, and they hold many secrets," says Roman. "The Quechua women from Larapata used to carry cloth bags like the one Elton has on, filled with potatoes, cassava, and other root vegetables, all the way to Pisac Market. They would start from here early in the morning and walk all day and into the night, descending into the Sacred Valley the following morning. Some still travel this way today."

Elton chimes in. "The women here live well into their 90s and beyond. When most Americans are slowing down in life at 80, the modern-day Incas walk these trails well into their golden years. It's what they know. It's what they live—a life of fortitude and close connection to nature."

And lots of potatoes.

■　■　■

The sun is making its way toward the mountain ridge that rims the valley across the Mapacho to the west as the five of us—our group now includes Anthony—descend through the highlands back toward the camp far below. The climb up, while physically demanding, was safe and controlled, but as I learned so intimately at the beginning of this trip, the way down is where the bulk of the danger lies on these Andean trails.

With the light quickly fading, we've decided to take a shortcut that should shave a good 30 minutes off our return trek to the base camp, but the narrow donkey path we're on is crumbling and hasn't been groomed in a long time.

Roman is leading the pack with his machete, slashing and hacking at the overhanging vines and branches that bar our passage, while we follow behind in single file. "Anthony hasn't had a chance to clear and repair this trail yet," Roman says, "so watch out—" As I lean in to hear what he's saying, the long blade zips through the air a few inches from my face as he draws it back to swipe at the tangle in front of him.

Roman continues swashbuckling as I turn around to see how close behind us the other three are. Mileen and Elton are both in sight, about 50 yards back, but there is no sign of Anthony. As Elton closes the brief distance between us, he calls out, reading my mind.

"Don't worry about our straggler," Elton says. "He's our resident wild man. Anthony must have seen something on the trail that needed tending to. If it weren't for him repairing these trails, we wouldn't have been able to get up to the top today."

Mileen and I look at each other, wide-eyed. One person managed to clear and rebuild that entire path?

We hear the quick pit-pat of footsteps on the switchback overhead, and within seconds Anthony is gliding down the trail toward us with a heavy backpack secured tightly around his shirtless torso. He's staring at the ground the entire way, chewing coca as he goes, lost in thought—or possibly entranced by the terrain. Judging by his exposed midsection, he has next to zero body fat and is able to maneuver down these ledges about twice as fast as we can.

"What are you guys waiting for? We're gonna be late for our final helping of quinoa and plantain mush!" Anthony grins, exposing a wad of coca tucked between cheek and molars.

The rest of our descent is fast. Compared with last night's blind trek, it's a cakewalk.

Every once in a while, Roman stops and points out a small carving in the hard rock mountain face that walls the left side of the path. These perfect trapezoids cut through stone are easy to miss because of the encroaching undergrowth, but once spotted they're truly remarkable to behold. And like many things in these mountains, they raise a lot of questions.

They are sacred deposit slots that have been used for thousands of years to give offerings to the apus, or mountain gods. Every mountain in the Andes is considered to be a living god with many powers, one of them being the power to give life or take it away. Coca leaves are generally the offering of choice. The traveler makes a kintu of three unblemished leaves, blows his or her prayers of protection and gratitude into them, and places the triad into the hole before proceeding on his or her journey. The more I investigate these traditions, the clearer it becomes that they imply a state of complete reverence for life itself and the need for constant expression of gratitude.

Archaeologists are still perplexed by the laserlike precision with which these geometric altars were carved. The offering slots are seen throughout the Peruvian Andes and date back more than 1,000 years, when humans in Europe were still defecating in holes and butchering one another using crudely crafted iron swords and armor. Meanwhile, tens of thousands of miles away, someone had the technology to cut these perfect shapes that run deep into the rock, sometimes with no measurable end.

I've seen similar cuts like this in the gargantuan walls that line the ancient roads of the Sacred Valley and Machu Pichu. With their precise edges, corners, and planes, they could only be created using tools developed in the 20th century or later, at least according to the commonly accepted history of civilization that is taught in most universities. But carbon dating doesn't lie. These "impossible" works have confounded archaeologists for the past century, and standing in front of one of the little openings right now sends a shiver down my spine. What did these people know that we have yet to unlock?

■ ■ ■

An hour later we're in the Paititi Institute's dining hall once again, stretching out tired limbs and staring down one last steaming bowl of quinoa and plantains. Anthony is already well into his second portion before I've had a full three bites.

It's 5 P.M., four hours until ceremony is supposed to start, and I'm starting to feel the jitters. The waiting hours leading up to ceremony are always the most difficult for me.

"Nick," says Roman, "you've got to eat something. When you purge tonight it will be a lot easier on your body if you have something in your stomach." Roman turns to Elton and Stella. "One thing I remember about Nick is that he purges quite a bit."

The three laugh with kind eyes directed at me. I smile, fighting off all the fear that is building around the words Roman speaks. Over the past 30 minutes of decreased physical activity, the fear has started reaching for me again, gnawing at my stomach. "Grandma has been calling to me ever since we ended our hike, *hermano*. I think I might purge before the ceremony even starts."

I do my best to get a few more bites down. To Roman's side sits Stella, one of his three apprentices, who also acts as the mother figure to all students and patients at the center. She has a gentleness about her that belies her punk-rock exterior. Her hair is buzzed short on one side and hangs down long and beautiful on the other, making her look like a warrior priestess straight out of a Mad Max film. Originally from Montreal, she speaks with a thick and beautiful French accent to the work-study permaculture students who are eating next to us.

They're not on the ayahuasca diet plan, and their food looks and smells delicious.

"As you all know," Roman says to the group, "the six of us will be having an ayahuasca ceremony in the chapel tonight, so Sasha will be in charge in the event of any urgent matters or questions until tomorrow morning." Sasha, a very kind-looking woman in her mid 40s, seems to be at ease with the responsibility laid at her feet—she has apparently done this before. She mops some mouthwatering jungle veggie stew from her bowl with a crunchy piece of homemade sourdough bread while she listens.

Sitting against a stucco wall next to Stella, Sasha tells Roman, "I've already had the team prepare the lemon and garlic water for you to have in the ceremony tonight. Do you need any other preparations made?"

"The only other thing we ask is that all music and other noise stop by 8:30 P.M.," says Roman. "And also, please do not open those chapel doors tonight unless it is a life-and-death emergency."

■ ■ ■

The shaman and his apprentices finish up their bowls of suste-nance with a casualness that I can't help but find distracting. It feels like this could be any other night for these four. Their expres-sions, tone of voice, and topic of conversation hold no trace of anticipation. The spiritual trial they are about to enter into doesn't seem to be the tiniest blip on their radar.

After downing his final spoonful, Roman stands up and walks across the large community structure to where Mileen and I sit. "It's now 5:30, and it would be a good idea for us all to go get some rest before ceremony."

I nod. "Sounds good. See you at the chapel in a few hours." In fact, this idea sounds like torture. There's no way in hell I'm going to sleep right now.

The shaman and his apprentices make a few more minutes of light conversation with the other residents and then exit into the dusk. Mileen turns to me. "Hey, are you going to head back to your tent?" he asks.

I do my best to look as unaffected as the four who just stepped out. "I think I'll stick around here for a little while. Not that tired."

"Okay. Well, I'm gonna head back and try to get some shut-eye. Sounds like we've got a long night ahead of us."

"Good idea. I'll be right behind you."

He places his plate, spoon, and cup in the dirty-dish bin, opens up the bug flap, and disappears into the woods.

I am now a lingerer. Open to any distraction.

One of the permaculture work-study students from across the room gives me a huge smile. "It's so cool to be sitting with you in person, man. I've seen *The Sacred Science* at least five times now, and it's the only reason I'm here today. I recognized you right when you walked in."

This twentysomething with a thick beard is the fifth per-son who has approached me in the past 24 hours, and like the other four, he is gushing with gratitude, as if I somehow have a mastery over the powerful healing traditions that were explored in the film.

Little does he know that I'm in a quiet, expertly masked, emotional tailspin, awaiting with dread what will befall me in the chapel in a few hours. I have one quivering pinky toe in the reality currently in front of me here in the Paititi dining hall.

"I'm so happy to hear that," I force myself to say. "What's your name again?"

"Sean."

"Sean, very nice to meet you, brother. My name is Nick. Where are you from?"

Sean tells me he's from Sacramento and that he recently dropped out of college because he didn't know what he wanted to do with himself. His family life is not good, and he really doesn't have any other place to go after this trip. Permaculture and living in true connection with nature have really opened up his eyes, he says, awakening a purpose inside him that he didn't realize was there.

"I'm hoping that Roman lets me sit in an ayahuasca ceremony while I'm here. I think it would really help me. How many times have you sat in ceremony, Nick?"

"This will be my sixth time, but I haven't worked with her in two years, and to be totally honest, I'm a little scared about this one." As soon as I admit it, I feel a sort of relief at having opened up about my fears. "You never know what you're going to get with Grandma. I've learned the hard way that it's best to prepare yourself for intensity before walking into the circle. The experience can be a beautiful and gentle journey, but I'd rather let that be a surprise."

A few more volunteers walk in with their aromatic plates of normal food. Listening in on their happy banter, these folks are about to enjoy a relaxing evening of reading by headlamp, practicing qigong massage techniques on one another, and ultimately falling into a cozy slumber at a reasonable hour.

We are polar opposites tonight. The knots are tightening in my stomach, and I decide it's probably best to leave. I bid everyone an awkward and abrupt adieu and find myself heading down the steep path to my tent in the fading sunlight.

What am I going to do for the next three hours? The only choice I have is the one I don't want: zip myself in my tent and try to get some sleep. Everyone else seems to be more than able to do this, so why not me? I bear left at a fork in the trail, then make a right at a painted stone on the ground that says "Jupiter" (my patron planet address for this visit to Paititi), demarcating my jungle quarters.

There she is, tucked beneath an enormous vilca tree in front of an old Incan retaining wall—my orange one-man Marmot tent.

Here goes nothing.

■ ■ ■

Lying in my sleeping bag, I'm doing a fairly good job of keeping my brain blank. My meditation machine is working, zapping thoughts as they try to get a foothold on me. The sounds of the forest outside, with the low, rumbling backdrop of the Mapacho River, are slowly washing away my fears, dissolving the separation between myself and the world around me.

This valley is magical. This land is medicine in itself.

Why do I even need to sit in ceremony, then? Just walking these trails, bathing in these waterfalls and streams, and having the Mapacho River itself close by are profoundly affecting my psyche. Heck, I had one of the most meaningful transformations of my life last night, just getting here.

Some tribes don't even let non-apprentices drink ayahuasca. Maybe they're right—this medicine isn't for the unanointed.

Just like that, the tranquility of my surroundings disappears, leaving in its wake a steam train of excuses and justifications, with a very special type of fear fueling the engine.

Why do I always do this to myself? I can't NOT go tonight. It's a special honor to be invited to sit with a shaman and his apprentices. What am I so afraid of? I know that ayahuasca doesn't kill. I'll survive this.

Crystal-clear memories of previous ceremonies and the hornet's nest of visual and aural chaos that rises around me not long after drinking a cup of ayahuasca begin to flood my awareness. It's normally impossible for me to conjure images and sensations from ceremonies gone by, which are usually beyond description and therefore hard to file away or relive. But now, as I stand on the precipice of yet another plunge into the primordial realm of Pachamama, I'm experiencing the sensations I have come to fear.

You are afraid because you lose yourself in the circle. It's one thing to see, feel, and hear disturbing things (demons, shadows, your own self-talk). But tumbling through the darkness, suffering without knowing who or what you are—that's a different kind of terror. It becomes so strong that you have to fight for each breath. And there's no escape once it starts.

I'm such an idiot for choosing this as my path. It's too hard. I'm not strong enough to endure this. It's only a matter of time before everyone sees me for what I really am.

I'm spinning out of control in my mummy sleeping bag, unable to calm myself down. A heavy sadness descends upon me, akin to the grief people on death row might feel on the eve of their execution, knowing they will never see their families again. Tears begin to flow, but sadness is better than fear, so I indulge it.

A voice in me makes a cutting observation. *Wow. You're really going through it right now. The ceremony has already begun, my friend.*

An image of my three-year-old son, River, shimmers to life behind my eyelids.

Remember who you are doing this work for, and why. You're willing to do whatever it takes to evolve and become the clear and loving person you were born into this world to be. This is why you are on this path—to dissolve the illusion, mend the wounds, and be your truth. Don't ever forget that.

When the fear comes, remember that you chose this. You are brave— that is your gift—but so is introspection, which is a cousin of self-doubt. Only you can choose which of these gifts you want to feed, and when.

It's not about me and it's all about me. The fear in my heart dissolves as this wisdom floods in and takes its place. I'm doing this in order to be a better, more connected human being. I'm not on death row—I'm walking consciously through a doorway of purification. The fear is a natural response, but the volume I play it at is my choice.

One of my biggest *why*s right now is River. I want to heal the unresolved blocks from my past so he doesn't have to deal with the ancestral traumas that were handed down to me. If he were watching me right now, I would be brave and not give this another thought. Done.

I reach toward the corner of my tent, finding my cell phone in the darkness. It flashes on, illuminating the tent. 7:36 P.M. I have 84 minutes until ceremony. Time to rest.

■　■　■

At the appointed time, I walk over to Mileen's tent, a green one-man North Face that is perched on an adjacent ledge looking out through the trees at the Mapacho River. He's already awake and hears my approach. "Time to go?" he asks quietly in the darkness.

"Ten to nine. We're right on time."

The tranquility has stuck over the past hour and a half and stays with me as we navigate our way via headlamp through the forest, passing the darkened jungle kitchen and dining hall on our way to the chapel.

The silhouette of the 500-year-old structure is outlined by a star-filled night sky. The door is just slightly ajar, the faint flicker of candlelight illuminating a slice of ground near the entrance.

To the right of the door is a small wooden sign that reads, "*No zapatos.*" No shoes. I fumble with my muddy hiking boots in the dark and catch the twinkle of two more headlamps moving through the woods above us.

As my foot crosses the old iron threshold, any shred of residual trepidation disintegrates. The table has been set, and fear is a waste of energy now.

The door creaks as Mileen opens it wider, stepping in behind me. A dimly lit figure is bent down lighting a few additional candles across the room.

"Welcome, you two." Stella stands up and gives us both a hug. "Roman and the others will be here in a few minutes. Mileen, that spot is for you, and that one over there is for you, Nick." She gestures toward a place on the blanketed floor against the hard adobe brick wall. Each spot has a cushion and a white bucket—the staples of an ayahuasca ceremony.

Mileen sits down against the opposite wall and closes his eyes as Stella lights one last candle before finding her own spot against the altar at the head of the room.

The door creaks open and in walk Elton and Anthony, whispering to each other excitedly about some new permaculture technique they've been trying out on one of the terraces. Their demeanor is light and lucid, like this is a routine part of their week.

Elton smiles down at me as he finds his spot across the room, next to Mileen. "Did you get some good sleep, brother?"

"Not really. I think the ceremony has already started for me."

"She works that way sometimes, no? I needed sleep after our hike today, though. I woke up a few minutes ago, just in time to start dreaming awake here with you all."

Anthony sits down cross-legged next me and nods hello before closing his eyes.

Stella begins to sing an ícaro softly to herself, and probably to us. "*Todo cura, todo sana, todo tiene medicina adentro de di di di. Llevo tierra adentro alli. Llevo fuego adentro de di di di. Tengo líneas dentro . . .*"

Still no jitters whatsoever. These settling-in moments are where I usually begin to get anxious, but everything is *tranquilo*. In the place of anxiety, there's a sense of kindredness and excitement for what's about to transpire in our little group. I feel honored to be here, and whatever is about to happen seems to be irrelevant to the flow I'm feeling right now.

"Good evening, everyone." Roman peeks his head in the door as he takes his hiking boots off outside. He crosses to the final vacant cushion, next to Stella, and does a quick survey of the room, making sure that everything is in order. Across one shoulder is a handwoven medicine bag, which he removes and places on the floor next to a couple of one-liter soda bottles filled with a cloudy, caramel-colored liquid.

"Tonight is a very auspicious evening. It's the full moon and the solstice at the same time. Many indigenous communities in these mountains will be waking up at 4 A.M. tomorrow morning to meet the sunrise."

It is called Inti Raymi. The celebration of the sun, the bright sun of our consciousness.

"It is quite appropriate that we are working with Grandmother Ayahuasca, who is the queen of the subconscious. She is going to help us purge any impurities that exist down there tonight so we can meet the sun anew tomorrow.

"Remember, our responsibility during the ceremony is to let her do her work and not interfere with the process. It's essential that we trust Mother Nature in whatever form she takes. The people of this land who are still connected to their ancestral traditions have an inherent trust in Pachamama because they have seen firsthand what she can do to heal their sick and bring wisdom when the way is unclear.

"For those of us who are not direct descendants of these lineages, this faith in the unknown sometimes takes a little work to build.

"Some Amazonian traditions consider ayahuasca to be a process of exorcism. She exorcises negative energies and obscurations of consciousness from our being so that life energy can begin to flow into those places again. What often is referred to in the normal understanding of exorcism as a demon or possession does not usually take this shape. More often it comes in the form of an uncomfortable sensation, tension, or disturbing emotion.

"In the next eight hours, it's important not to amplify the tensions that might come up for you. If you cannot relax with something you are experiencing, then relaxing with your inability to relax is the lesson to master.

"It's good to purge outside, but just be careful not to go too far. There are precipices outside the chapel, so be mindful of where you step."

Elton raises his hand and Roman nods to him. The apprentice clears his throat and adds, "And also the fairy, just in case she comes."

"Oh, yes. Do you want to say something about that, Elton?"

Elton continues in his Maltese accent. "Just in case the fairy comes—sometimes she comes—don't follow her, because it can be very dangerous. She can fly, but remember that we humans have not developed the wings to fly through open space without getting hurt, so please be realistic with your physical limitations. If anyone is calling and it is not Roman or one of the rest of us, please do not follow."

"And just to avoid confusion, our voices tend to come from within the chapel," Roman adds, peering at us over his thin-rimmed glasses.

The apprentices laugh, but I can't tell whether the fairy thing is a joke or not. I'll just let that extra bit of information go for now.

"I'm already struggling tonight, so I am going to forgo any further formalities and begin the ceremony. Does anyone have any questions before we start?"

We all look at one another, smiles creasing our faces involuntarily. Spirit brothers and sisters. Home.

Roman produces a few more items from his sack: a small ceramic cup, his flute, a bundle of palo santo sticks, some mapacho tobacco, and a tied bundle of dried leaves known in the Shipibo tradition as a *chakapa*. This fan-shaped instrument is shaken in a constant rhythm on and around a patient during a *limpia*, or healing intervention. It is said that the leaves trap the bad spirits as they exit the body and are later purified in the forest. Maybe that's where the fairies come in. Maybe this is all a load of twisted shamanic humor. Either way, here we are.

I'm the second to receive a cup of medicine. Roman smiles at me before he pours it. "It's good to have you back, Nick." A few quick blessings and a waft of palo santo smoke and the medicine is in my body.

Five minutes later, the initial gag reflex has passed and the weight of the dense liquid is sitting inside my stomach. It's only a matter of time now.

Roman fills a final cup and says a quick prayer, looks up at the rest of us, and says, *"Salud,"* before downing it in one gulp.

The shaman leans forward toward the last lit candle in the room and says, "Remember, when you fear the monsters and demons you become one yourself. Monsters are drawn to other monsters, so fear will only bring more your way. Don't cling to or resist anything you are about to encounter. There is no good or bad."

He brings the candle up to his face and blows it out.

Black.

■　■　■

I'm staring into the darkness, welcoming anything that floats in.

Remember, self, there are three tools available to you if things get too intense.

One is temperature control. Cold air always helps ground me when I've gone too far. Removal of my shirt may be required. It's a cool night, and the two layers I have on—hoodie and T-shirt—still feel okay.

Two is water. After a strong purge, a little water can help cool the system and remind me that I'm a physical being with a throat and a digestive system. It can also induce a purge that is waiting to come out.

Three is breath. The worst thing to do is forget to breathe, but sometimes I do. *Don't do that tonight.*

My hands and feet start to tingle. Here it comes.

Stella is singing an ícaro that seemed pretty and perfect a few moments ago, but each syllable is now starting to penetrate. The tingling has stopped and there is no bodily disintegration or feeling of weightless disorientation. I'm still here, but somehow I am also somewhere else in the room, looking over at myself with clear sight.

The me in me is still there, but there is another me outside, observing the physical meat suit that is me. This man is nearing 40 and trying so hard to be the most ideal version of himself according to some predetermined set of rules, trying so hard to hold on to it all. Cracking the whip, depriving himself of peace for fear that if he lets go, his life will fall away and be wasted.

What does that mean—wasted? Is there someone keeping score, making sure Nick behaves himself and contributes everything he has to the world? *Who matters most—the world or your family? Have you been good to them lately? Does this self-deprivation make you more at ease around River?*

An image of my son running into my office while I'm working flashes through the darkness. I scold him and tell him he knows he's not supposed to open my door while I'm working. His mom takes him by the hand and leads him away.

No.

This Nick fellow who is sitting against the wall, holding on to make sure his bowels don't spill their contents across the chapel floor, is definitely on the path, but he's still holding on to some serious shadows from his childhood. Catholic fear patterns combined with unresolved self-worth issues from a bumpy 12 years in a suburban school system. He's so dedicated to making this life count that he forgets to toss in the towel when it's time to play and be free.

Time to peel away the next membrane of your psyche and awaken the free-spirited child who rises each day with wonder and fearlessness. You will never be able to love your wife and children fully if you don't.

Let the medicine in.

The ícaro has ended and I'm sobbing in the darkness. The cosmic bitch slap that I've been dreading the past few days never arrived. In its place was about 10 years of psychotherapy delivered in a quasi-out-of-body experience. In the few minutes of separation from the mental meat suit that calls itself Nick, the real me diagnosed the imbalance and prescribed the remedy.

Give yourself some breathing room to mess up. Otherwise you'll choke off the essence, burn yourself out, and worst of all, not have fun.

Man, I really am way too hard on myself. How did I miss that?

Don't start being hard on yourself for being too hard on yourself. This guilt rap is a circle trap, see? You can't think your way out of this mess. You need to tap into your flow and feel your way back there whenever you fall out of it.

I don't need to tell you not to drink drain cleaner, right? It's poison, so you're careful with it. Well, guilt is poison. Shame is poison. It feeds on itself and begets more of the same, which is why you're on this path—to end the cycle, expose it and release it.

My hand is wrapped around one knee as I fight off the discomfort of an inevitable purge. Realizing that I'm depriving myself of this core biological need for fear of disrupting the ceremony by creaking open the heavy metal door, I find myself standing up. *Stop the bullshit, Nick. Take care of your needs.*

I yank the door handle and walk out into the night.

The Mapacho rapids roar down below as I step down a twisted path toward the bathroom stalls via headlamp. It feels magical to be walking through the forest under a night sky, illuminated by a rare summer-solstice full moon. Maybe I'll just wander these trails for a while after I do my business.

Oh yeah, the fairies. Best to heed the advice of the locals, no matter how much it offends my rationalist sensibilities.

A few moments later I'm back in the chapel, returning to my spot on the floor.

Elton is singing an ícaro in a Quechua dialect. The melody floats up and down, dancing through the darkness in front of us, and my mouth begins to move, voicing the sounds I'm hearing. The tones become mine, finding their way into every nook and cranny of my psyche, prodding and poking at areas of resistance. The volume of the low rumblings coming from my vocal cords begins to amplify as I join Elton, and now Roman and Stella, in the same ícaro.

Grandma is here in full force, but in a form different from what I've ever experienced. No visual or existential shock and awe whatsoever, but instead moments of deep sorrow that beckon me down to their roots. Singing with the shaman and his apprentices, I'm exposing subtle levels of stagnation that I've been blind to until now.

The sadness feels good.

A few hours later, as the faint blue light of dawn begins to peak underneath the chapel door, a blunt question is posed by the medicine.

Why are you always so afraid to come see me? You never regret it.

All the fear, the expectation of discomfort, the preparation for doom was your medicine tonight. The ceremony was just a prop to shine a light on the way you torment yourself.

The world is full of unknowns, but the one thing you can determine amid it all is how you are going to relate to yourself.

Never forget that you are your own strongest ally.

10 MEDICINE QUESTIONS

If you're wrestling with a bit of work that just doesn't want to reveal its medicine to you, here is a list of questions you can ask yourself that might help reveal some inroads to the essence. But remember, these obstacles are like the Andes Mountains. Once you summit one, you will then see the seemingly infinite number of mountains that surround you in every direction, just waiting to be climbed.

The mission is not to conquer them all, but to learn to love the climb. Every handhold, every hidden alpine meadow, every crag and cliff, the fear you feel when you look down, the exhilaration you know is waiting for you at the top. Stay open to every piece of information that comes to you.

A small disclaimer: Some of these questions might seem a little heavy. No need to "go there" if it doesn't feel right at this moment.

There are no right or wrong answers to any of them. The intention with these questions is to help you define the coastlines, mountains, and valleys of your inner landscape. Before working with them, it's a good idea to sit peacefully for a few minutes and allow the ticker tape of thought to quiet down.

1. Is there any tension or pain in my body right now? If I could give it a name, what would I call this sensation?

2. What is the one thing my body needs right now that I haven't been giving it?

3. What is preventing me from being peaceful/happy/content right this moment? (If it's something material, what feeling or relief would that material thing bring me?)

4. When was the last time I did something that put me outside my comfort zone? What was it, and what was my motivation for doing it? What have I not been doing in my life that would give me that same feeling?

5. What is the one difficult conversation that I've been putting off having with my mother, my father, or a close loved one?

6. What is the one difficult conversation that I've been putting off having with myself?

7. What was the last white lie I told? Who did I tell it to? Why did I tell it? What would have happened if I had told the truth? (If the term "white lie" doesn't resonate with you, think instead about a time you exaggerated or minimized something you told someone.)

8a. What is one thing I haven't forgiven myself for?

8b. Is there a person in my life who I haven't fully forgiven? How did this person wrong me? What is stopping me from forgiving him or her right now?

9. Years from now, when I am breathing my final breaths, what advice would I give the "now me"?

10. Who am I? (Who is seeing through these eyes, who is hearing through these ears? What defines me at the center of my consciousness?)

Chapter 14

◇◇◇◇◇◇◇◇◇◇◇◇◇◇

DEPARTURE

We are not separate. Rather, we are connected to one source and to a web of life. Imagine a hand where one of the fingers drops to the floor and thinks it can have an independent life without being connected to the body. That is what is happening today. Humankind is acting like separate fingers that have forgotten the connection to the original source of life.

—Sandra Ingerman

June 24, 2016
Larapata, Peru

It's Friday morning, and I'm following Roman and Elton around the crowded San Pedro Market in central Cusco. They have a two-page shopping list that was given to them by the folks at the Land, who have requested both materials for the center and items for personal use.

Today is the last day of my trip, and I've decided to spend it helping Roman and Elton shop. My flight back to San Francisco departs in four hours, so I might as well do something productive to fill the time.

Ducking and weaving between stalls of potions, produce, and power tools, we make our way through the maze of merchants, stopping here and there to haggle and purchase. We walk into the open doorway of a mattress merchant, hoping to cross one of the heftiest items off the list—five beds for the new healing dieta huts that are being built back at Paititi. As Roman pokes and prods at different plastic-wrapped mattresses and makes observations about the pricing and quality that are clearly intended to help his negotiating position, my mind begins to wander to what life will be like when I get back home.

On these excursions into the sacred outback of South and Central America, your rigid patterning around the daily grind of modern life gradually (or sometimes not so gradually) tends to fall away. The illusions that you've built up around you are challenged right from the outset, their origins and toxic effects becoming painfully apparent. After a few weeks of immersion and surrender, the volume on these neurotic impulses is dialed down and sometimes goes away completely. In its place come happiness, simplicity, purpose, and peace.

During the spans of time in between these adventures, as I reimmerse myself in the modern world, I try to be as conscious as I can about keeping alive inside me the ancestral way of being that permeates these native cultures. There are usually one or two major "rearrangements" to the structure of my life when I get back to the States, intended to make my world more congruent with my highest ideals.

It's sometimes as simple as repositioning or removing objects that are stagnant in my living space or adding an abalone shell to my kitchen counter to remind me to make more sage/palo santo offerings in the morning. But these adjustments are often more intrapersonal, like sitting down with a dear friend or lover and sharing an epiphany about the way you've been interacting with each other. Conversations like this can lead to the formation of a new sacred contract, like "I now understand *this* about myself, and if you see me embodying *that* negative belief or disposition, I give you full permission to communicate it to me directly."

The more intimate readjustments are the hardest, but they tend to endure the test of time with lasting impact.

But staying immersed in the more elusive *way of being*, the essence of what I felt while gliding gracefully down a precarious Incan trail in the dark of night, is hard to hold in the modern world.

Until this recent expedition, I had caught only momentary glimpses of this realm of consciousness, usually at the pinnacle of a plant medicine ceremony. But something has shifted in my late-night coca ceremonies with Roman, and I'm now in semiconstant connection with it.

The imperceptible disappearance or dissipation of this feeling is actually the most insidious part of returning. If it were stripped away in a violent instant upon setting foot back in California, it would at least be obvious enough to make some decisions around. But it isn't this way.

The essence sometimes continues to shine, fully intact, for days and weeks as I navigate my old life with clear sight, building and repairing relationships and my orientation toward my surroundings with full presence. Only over time do I begin to feel this wholeness diminish like a lantern burning up its final few drops of oil, replaced by unexplainable plummets in peacefulness and the usual substitutes for deeper life flow—like coffee, alcohol, the consumption of mainstream media.

Something that Roman said keeps flashing through my mind as I anticipate this conundrum. When I got here a few weeks ago, still reeking of the modern world, he gently observed that the thoughts and behaviors I was conveying held an imprint of perceived separation.

"Nick," he said, "this notion of a private and separate internality that is at odds with a perceived externality is part of the disease of the Western world."

I was convinced that I was Nick and the rest of the world was external to me. I was operating as if my thoughts and emotions existed only within me and had no impact on the outside world, other than those that compelled me into physical action.

But this is clearly a fallacy, as evidenced by what happened to the film crew and me while we were making *The Sacred Science*. Though we tried to maintain a professional distance, all five of us were sucked into the same existential supernova that our jungle patients were experiencing. We realized the hard way that our intentions and internal dialogues were not safely stowed away back in the States, waiting to greet us upon our return.

There is no way to stay on the sidelines if you want to engage fully with the world around you. There is no insulation between your consciousness, your intentions, and the energy you are projecting toward the people and events around you; there is only lack of awareness of this. Being present in your own reality is not just some abstract shamanic state of enlightenment. It's a state of essential honesty, with ourselves and the world around us, that we humans should be aspiring to every day—whether that day is spent on a wooden boat headed down the Ucayali River or in a mundane office cubicle.

The distraction of our immediate surroundings is just an illusion, something that tempts us to ignore the story of who we really are.

I recall another conversation I had with Roman just a few nights ago, during a coca ceremony, when it occurred to me that when I returned to the States, I was going to have a very hard time holding on to the soul upgrade he had given me.

"I wish I could move my entire family down here so we could all live in this way," I said.

"Live in what way?" he asked.

"You know, with deeper connection to who we actually are in each moment. Real conversations and sense of tribe," I tried to explain.

"How come you can't do that where you live?" he asked.

"I want to, but it's so hard. My folks and a lot of my friends don't understand what I'm doing down here. They think I'm nuts."

"That, brother, is the work," he said. "Your work. Don't make the mistake of attaching what you've experienced here to any time or place. This experience is available to you anywhere you go, it's just a matter of learning how to tap into it.

"There is no magical place to do this work," he said. "You and I happen to be in Peru, but the entire world is our training ground. Remember, no matter where you go, there you are."

The sound of Roman's bartering in the market shakes me from my thoughts for a second. "I'll take three of the single mattresses," he is saying, "but we need them to be foam, not feather. Nick, you wanted an alpaca blanket to bring back with you, right? Those ones over there are of really high craftsmanship."

Seeing Roman haggling with a vendor over the price of mattresses reminds me that even he is not fully isolated from the mundane details of modern life. As I wander through the crammed bedding shop toward the blankets he suggested, I wonder again what it is that keeps derailing me from maintaining the way of being I learned in the Amazon when I get back home.

This time the answer comes back at me almost instantaneously. *I have a lack of trust in the people in my life back home, and a base fear that if I stop actively willing things to happen, I won't be able to provide for my family.*

These two things are central to our way of life in the Western world. We grow up knowing that we'll be booted out of the house at age 18, maybe to college or straight into the workforce to begin fending for ourselves. If we're "successful" we wind up being able to afford our own homes, with our own fenced-off turf, allowing us space—or separation—from everyone else, including our own families. This is the foundation of the American Dream, but it comes with a hefty price tag.

We are taught to work as hard and ferociously as we can, to excel in our given occupations, so that we can stockpile some cash to pay the mortgage or rent, student loan, day care, health insurance, life insurance if we're lucky, phone bill, car loan, and hopefully have something left to buy groceries.

Our culture pushes us to have one hell of a convincing backstory in order to inspire trust and earn greater responsibilities—i.e., good jobs. If we're good enough at learning the Western game of survival, separation, and competition, we get to have higher-quality stuff and heightened protection from the elements, disease, hunger, and the criminal justice system. This in turn feeds an inner emptiness that we know no way to mitigate except with more of the same.

I was no different when I first began this seeker's search. I had an innate curiosity about the subject I was investigating but a naive expectation that I'd be able to film these cultures objectively, remaining untouched by the magico-religious interventions they use.

But before I was ever granted access to film anything, I underwent a series of rituals that shattered everything I knew myself to be.

After the initial terror of seeing it all stripped away so easily, followed by the abyss of realizing that I did not know, nor had I ever really known, who I was or what this reality we live in is, I was able to reconstruct something new with the shards of shattered me that remained on the floor. Something more aware—of the fallacies inherent in the Western ethos and of the truths that lie beyond.

But like everything else in this world, the new me that stepped out of these healing rites wasn't and isn't permanent. I've earned the trust of a shaman or two, and this has opened the door to further contacts and invitations to continue the journey. But over the course of these past few years, new illusions—subtler this time around—have begun to cling and cluster around the core of the essential Nick, as evidenced by the new level of inner work that was laid before me in the chapel on the night of my last ayahuasca ceremony.

Every time the slate is cleaned, it's only a matter of time before new and improved story lines of sabotage gradually take hold. They're a universal constant, a self-impairing feature of the human mind.

I'm starting to identify these shadows as any attachment or resistance to an unforeseeable outcome. These thought forms appear reasonable and helpful to have but tear us out of the present moment, turning us into busy-brained, prattling monkeys.

I pretend to closely examine the barrel of alpaca blankets Roman pointed to, but my head is elsewhere, witnessing all the patterns that have been shed this time around.

Nothing matters but the way of being. Remember that it's always there if you just let the rest of the thought constructs drop away.

Eyes on the path, not on the edge.

■ ■ ■

A few hours later, I sit at my gate in the Alejandro Velasco Astete International Airport, feeling the dissonance caused by the familiar Western-style surrounds of a modern travel hub while still technically on the ground in Peru.

I wonder how many months I'll be able to hold on to the state of clarity I feel right now. It's more than a living meditation—it's an expansive, childlike contentedness paired with deeper intelligence. Everything makes sense. I can see the trajectory my life has taken to get me to this very moment, every event that is currently transpiring, and the future I envision for myself. It's all as plain as day.

I don't want to lose this again.

I undo my backpack straps and pull out my trusty Moleskine pocket notepad and a ballpoint pen. I am going to create a protocol for myself to follow. I know the core mission: nurture and embody this way of being, no matter where I am.

My newly proposed soul survival formula will be aimed at keeping me on the straight and narrow spirit path even in the concrete jungles and strip-malled towns of the Western world.

I begin taking inventory of the lessons I've learned in the Amazon and the Andes, noting the practices that Roman and the other shamans turned to in order to keep themselves centered and vibrant in times of intensity.

This list sprouts more lists, which will turn into days of research and refinement, ultimately shaping into some modus operandi that I'll use to guide the rest of my life.

The personal journey I propose to you is as epic and ancient as the Amazon rain forest itself and appears in the literature of pretty much every world culture. It starts with separation or departure; then come the trials and resulting wisdom of initiation; and finally there is the return and reintegration into society with a more complete understanding of oneself and one's place in the world.

But to that I will add one more thing: You don't need to go anywhere to experience this journey. There is no expensive plane ticket, time taken off from work, or hefty shopping spree at the wilderness apparel store. It may not be as romantic or outwardly glamorous as a trip to the jungle, but it can have an even greater impact on your life.

The eight patients we brought down to the Amazon were extremely sick, but on a soul level, the core problems they were working to resolve were nothing different from those we all experience in our own lives: attachment to our story, detachment from our true selves, stagnation due to stale patterns of thought that aren't serving us, fear of what others might think, fear of who we truly are inside, aversion to being vulnerable, lack of trust in ourselves and others, and ultimately, fear of the impermanence of it all—that is, fear of death.

The good news is that these seemingly toxic orientations toward our reality are 100 percent *human*. The tough news is that they must be acknowledged, understood, and dissolved in order for us to be healthy and benefit from the underlying wisdom they hold.

We can go to the ends of the earth to work on these things, but unless we as individuals are willing to show up right *now* and make the choice to be good to ourselves and do what we know is in alignment with our highest ideals, there isn't a shaman in the world who can save us.

As a father of two now, I don't have enough time and flexibility in my life to run down to the jungle every time I need a dose of Pachamama essence, so I operate on the basis of a few core principles that help me see the medicine path no matter where I am.

As you've probably surmised from the preceding chapters, this approach isn't a quick fix. Unfortunately, nothing truly valuable comes easy. This work is a moving tapestry, woven from ancient and present wisdom that can drastically change your life, but it takes perseverance and practice.

Patience is the first lesson on any spirit path. One of the hardest things to learn is that there will never be a moment when you will feel like you've finally arrived. As soon as you crest one mountain, you always see just far enough to get a glimpse of others that have yet to be summited.

This understanding can be a little deflating, once it really sinks in. *What is there to aim for if all my labor only adds up to more challenges?*

If you think about it, this concept of striving to achieve some far-off dream is sewn into the fabric of modern reality. It's the notion that we just need to hold our breaths a little bit longer, tolerate self-imposed stress for a few more months, years, or decades, until the payoff comes. We're mortgaging our very existence to some illusion of a happier future that we hope will become real once we've paid off all the debt.

It's a moving mirage that tricks us as we stagger across the desert, thirsty and tired. The oasis is not a lie. It does exist. But it isn't where we think it is.

The true reward is about cultivating a real but entirely metaphysical space between ourselves and the outside world. It's about realizing that there is room in each moment for you to be nurtured and thrive within, maintaining clear-sightedness no matter what life situation you encounter.

This is earth wisdom. As long as you live and breathe on this planet, you have access to it. It isn't native to any one ancient tradition, but is a core belief of many sacred ancestral disciplines worldwide.

Walking the healing path is a matter of endurance, and if we treat it like a sprint race, we're going to find ourselves overwhelmed and burned out. Members of the Tarahumara tribe in Mexico run 100 miles at a time, but not as a competition. They do it as part of a celebration. They aren't hoping the run is going to end—it's just the opposite. They learn to live and find joy in each step along the way.

Long-distance runners, rock climbers, and other endurance athletes often have to overcome many inner demons to allow their bodies to do the impossible. That is what the practices at the end of this chapter are intended to do on a spiritual level—show you the unthinkable so you can achieve the impossible.

Take a deep breath, hydrate, and settle in. Stepping onto the path itself is your solace.

If you are on it, you've already arrived.

YOUR SPIRITUAL TRAINING GROUND

What would happen if you reenvisioned your life and everything in it as a spiritual training ground? If, instead of looking at each day, each minute, each moment as something to get through until the easy part comes, you began to take a tally of how you are engaging with every circumstance you encounter, no matter how subtle or substantial.

How much of the real you are you offering to yourself and those you interact with? Where are you getting derailed? Where are you excelling?

It doesn't matter how old we get; playing games is something we humans just can't get enough of. Why not make a little game out of this serious thing we call life?

Don't worry—this doesn't require any more technology than you have with you. All you need is your body, your mind, your consciousness, and anything the outside world brings you.

If life were a game, what would your benchmarks of winning be? Mine would be growth, service, love, wisdom, excitement, and sense of tribe. You're welcome to borrow mine or come up with your own.

What would an indicator of losing be? The top candidates for me are feelings of shame, anger, ignorance, complacency, and stress. I left out fear and frustration because these are natural emotions, especially when we're pushing past our comfort zones. (Frustration is tricky because it can turn into anger or shame if we're not careful, but in its pure form it can be fuel for change.)

When setting the gauges on your internal dashboard, just make sure to be honest with yourself about what your own personal metrics are for a fulfilling and joyful life.

MISSION 1: NOTICE

Once you have both the goals and areas of derailment set, the rest is easy. Start walking through your life, trying to stay fully aware of how you're engaging with your surroundings. The goals are really there as a target status quo—how you want your life to be. Consider them to be cairns on a hiking trail, stacks of rocks that show you that you're on the right path.

But we also need to be aware of the cliffs and rock slides, so we'll be checking in with that internal index card of emotional pitfalls as we walk through each day—not because we're trying to avoid them, but to begin charting the various emotions and corresponding thoughts that light up in given circumstances.

We can't extract the wisdom from a challenge if we don't acknowledge it is occurring. Many of us have so many shields, safeguards, and backroom deals with ourselves that the act of simply *noticing* the triggers as they occur is a hefty task in itself.

If you are reading this book one page at a time, in a linear fashion, you read my words about the way of being earlier in this chapter. This state is available to all of us, and often it's there with us when we wake up in the morning, before the curveballs of life begin to fly.

Assuming we start off our days at zero, neither negative or positive, ask yourself, *Where is my essential, fully connected state getting derailed throughout my day?*

Have you ever had one of those days that begin beautifully, but by midafternoon you're a ball of nerves, checking in for the next flight to Crazytown? Looking back, it's often hard to even pinpoint what went wrong and when. But this is exactly where the medicine lies.

Like the 24 still photographs that make up each second of film you watch in a "motion picture," each moment of our lives holds an incredible amount of information. It might seem basic, but the ability to notice the subtleties of our experience in each moment is the door to personal evolution.

MISSION 2: REMEMBER

A self-sabotaging mechanism that we humans come conveniently equipped with is forgetfulness. This is advantageous when it comes to letting go and moving beyond traumatic events from our past, but sometimes it can get in the way of our spiritual growth. It's one thing to notice when you're being derailed from your essential state, but *remembering* the incident so it can be worked on at a later time is where a lot of us falter.

Don't dwell. Don't obsess. Just remember.

MISSION 3: MAKE A LIST

Now that you have your special X-ray spiritual training glasses on and you're walking bravely through the cosmic obstacle course of life, it's time to start making a list of the particular points of challenge that you're noticing.

Again, we're not talking about external challenges like a flat tire, parking ticket, or cracked windshield here. (Apparently my negatives are all car-related. Note to self: the reader knows too much.) Outer life disturbances are going to happen; that's the universal constant you can always set your watch to. But how are you reacting to each one? This is what will decide whether it makes the list.

What happened to you today that elicited a disproportionate emotional response? Where did you feel a negative surge of emotion well up that was beyond your control? Or just the opposite: did something occur today that should have birthed a negative or positive emotion but didn't? Sometimes numbness or a lack of feeling in response to an external event can be just as significant.

Be careful not to be tricked by the spackle and paint that your ego slaps on the shadows and cracks in your psyche. Unless you're a newborn child, I guarantee you have sore spots in there. Inner bruises come with living on this planet, and there's absolutely nothing wrong with them, as long as they are seen, mended, and used as portals for growth.

MISSION 4: FIND THE MEDICINE

This entire framework is centered on the shamanic principle that *everything* is medicine. It doesn't matter how painful, terrifying, or unpleasant the experience is—the master has learned how to transform these externalities into wisdom and fuel for greater spaciousness and compassion.

Think of it as inoculation against infectious disease. By exposing ourselves to circumstances that trigger a negative response in our pain-body, we allow our organism to build up spiritual and psychological immunity to future run-ins with these particular scenarios. But if we avoid taking our medicine or overdo it with the dose, we stay stunted and complacent.

How do you find the medicine? This is one of the hardest tasks on the spirit path.

So you're open, you're noticing the subtlety, and you just got triggered for the seventh time today by the same thing. You know this interaction is your kryptonite and it's an unavoidable part of your reality, but the lesson or hidden wisdom is not revealing itself to you.

Well, first off, congratulations on being awake! That's at least half the battle.

As Roman would say, this is the work, my friend. We moderners are living in the age of the quick fix, born into a culture of convenience where everything is or should be solvable in a fast and painless jiffy. Everything is speeding up—faster, better, more productive—while the quality of our interactions with others and ourselves is withering away on the vine.

People don't know who or what in the hell they are anymore. Most of us still think we're our names. Think about that for a second. If you ask a typical earth-dweller who they are, nine times out of ten they will tell you their name.

Well, I sure as hell am not Nick. I'm a shitload more and a shitload less. I'm an unquantifiable, flesh-encapsulated amalgamation of life force. I'm a temporary channel for the anonymous, unrefined driver of consciousness, flowing in through the heart, up to the brain and then downward through neurological pathways into the hand of the meat suit known as Nick—who is writing this book to awaken itself in you, the reader. (Did it work?)

It takes a lot to step up and look your own work right in the eye. There will always be more to do once this bit is done, so a little advice: cultivate patience. Slow down and relax into the experience you're currently having. The medicine will find you when it's ready.

■　■　■

When we begin to see each day as a personalized menu of opportunity for our unique spiritual evolution, the challenges and hiccups (which will never stop, by the way) take on a whole new meaning. They become perfect portions of exactly what you need to continue healing and strengthening the inner muscles, namely *patience, compassion, connection,* and *presence.*

How do you know if you've leveled up? Simple. Can you remain undistracted and present in the face of the same challenge tomorrow? If so, on to the next bit of work.

If not, failure is the best way to learn. Remember the Japanese proverb: *Fall seven times; stand up eight.*

EPILOGUE

If you've made it to this page, I thank you for giving my words your presence. Every moment in our lives is precious, and I'd like to pay you back with a pearl from one of the wisest souls I know, my five-year-old son, River.

I thought I knew something about life until I had a child. Roman once warned me that raising a family is the most powerful evolutionary medicine on the planet. Well, he wasn't joking. This kid has been schooling me since he got here.

I'm in River's bedroom tent one night, and we're doing our usual pre-slumber routine of thanking Pachamama for our life, for each other, and for everything she's given us. He stops midsentence, turns to me, and asks, "Dad, why do we say amen after we say the grateful things to Pachamama?"

"Because it helps us send our prayers up to God and the universe."

"What is God?"

"God is the big bright light that we all came from and that we're all going to."

"Like the moon?"

"Kind of, but different. God is the light that we all have inside us that makes us who we are."

"You mean like love?"

"Yes! God is love."

He stares into my eyes for a good minute, saying nothing, transmitting something I'll never be able to categorize or give name to.

His eyes widen and he lets out a giggle that quickly morphs into a yawn.

"Good night, Dad. I'm going to leave my light on, okay?"

BIBLIOGRAPHY

Arvigo, Rosita. *Sastun: My Apprenticeship with a Maya Healer*. New York: HarperCollins, 1994.

Beyer, Stephan. *Singing to the Plants: A Guide to Mestizo Shamanism in the Upper Amazon*. Albuquerque: University of New Mexico Press, 2009.

Buhner, Stephen Harrod. *Plant Intelligence and the Imaginal Realm: Beyond the Doors of Perception into the Dreaming of Earth*. Rochester, Vermont: Bear & Company, 2014.

Eliade, Mircea. *Shamanism: Archaic Techniques of Ecstasy*. Princeton, New Jersey: Princeton University Press, 1964.

Ermakov, Dmitry. *Bø and Bön: Ancient Shamanic Traditions of Siberia and Tibet in Their Relation to the Teachings of a Central Asian Buddha*. Frederick, Maryland: Vajra, 2008.

Gorman, Peter. *Ayahuasca in My Blood: 25 Years of Medicine Dreaming*. Charleston, South Carolina: CreateSpace, 2010.

Harner, Michael. *The Way of the Shaman: A Guide to Power and Healing*. New York: Harper & Row, 1980.

Ingerman, Sandra. *Soul Retrieval: Mending the Fragmented Self*. New York: HarperOne, 1991.

Kalweit, Holger. *Shamans, Healers and Medicine Men*. Boulder, Colorado: Shambala, 1992.

Kovacic, Peter and Ratnasamy Somanathan. "Novel, Unifying Mechanism for Mescaline in the Central Nervous System," *Oxidative Medicine and Cellular Longevity* 2, no. 4 (2009): 181–190.

Langdon, E. Jean Matteson. *Portals of Power: Shamanism in South America*. Albuquerque: University of New Mexico Press, 1992.

Pendell, Dale. *Pharmako Gnosis: Plant Teachers and the Poison Path*. Berkeley: North Atlantic Books, 2005.

Plotkin, Mark. *Medicine Quest: In Search of Nature's Healing Secrets*. New York: Viking, 2000.

Randall, Robert. "Qoyllur Rite, an Inca Fiesta of the Pleiades: Reflections on Time and Space in the Andean World," *Bulletin de l'Institut francais d'études Andins* 11 (1982).

Schultes, Richard Evans. *Plants of the Gods: Origins of Hallucinogenic Use*. New York: McGraw-Hill, 1979.

Taylor, Bron, ed. *Encyclopedia of Religion and Nature*. New York: Bloomsbury Academic, 2005.

INDEX

A

Addiction, 158

Alberto, 71, 103–104, 106–107

Aloe-based herb poultices, 83

Amazon rain forest

"everything is medicine" approach in, 158, 135–136

as filming location, 32–33, 71, 74, 102–103

as medicine, 59–62, 74–75, 92–93, 100, 101–102, 189

medicine walk in, 83–87

Anadenanthera colubrina trees, 142, 165–166, 189

Andean cactus, 48, 137–141, 142, 145–146, 166, 181

Angel trumpet, 98, 141–143

Anger, 102, 160–163, 211

Animal spirits, 146, 166

Anthony, 11, 18, 181–184, 192

Arthritis, 67, 84

Arturo, 1–3

Ayahuasca

animal spirit of, 166

as feminine archetype, 37, 45–46, 137–138, 193

ingredients of, 105

medicinal properties of, 19, 36–37, 95–96

story of, 35–36

as teacher plant, 142

Ayahuasca ceremonies

advice and warnings for, 37, 39, 59

author's dread of, 18–19, 38–42, 179–180, 185–191

author's experience of, 38–49, 188, 190, 192–198

dieta and, 83

digestive system, effect on, 36–37, 95–96

letting go during, 42–48

pendulum of experiences during, 47–48, 197–198

post-ceremony connections, 49–50

preparation for, 177–178, 180, 186

    purging during, 19, 39, 43–44

    purpose of, 58

    shaman film candidates at, 62–64

    for shaman initiation, 85–86

Ayahuasca toffee, 41–42

B

Banisteriopsis caapi vine, 105

Banya, 53–54

Blocks

    author's personal, 18, 27, 52, 160–163, 191

    distractions as, 72–73, 75–79, 105–106, 152, 172–173

    emotional, 139

    techniques for removing, 98, 139, 163, 167–168

Breast cancer, 83, 84, 152–153

Brock, 71, 107, 111–112, 124, 153

Brugmansia grandiflora (toé), 98, 141–143

C

Cactus (Andean), 48, 137–141, 142, 145–146, 166, 181

Cancer, 68, 76, 83, 84, 99–102, 111–115, 145–147, 152–155

Candy (ayahuasca toffee), 41–42

Catholicism, 16, 21–23, 196

Ceremonies

    ayahuasca. *See* Ayahuasca ceremonies

    clearing, 119–120

closing ceremony for retreat, 157–160

coca, 15–19, 125–131, 134, 160–163, 203, 204–205

    San Pedro, 137–141, 144–148, 154

Chakapa, 194

Chapels, 15–16, 191

Charlatans, 68–70

Chemotherapy, 153

Chiric sanango, 98

Chorisia integrifolia (lupuna), 85–87

Christian, 83–87, 158

Chuchuhuasi, 84

Clarity. *See* Consciousness

Clearing ceremonies, 119–120

Closing ceremony, for retreat, 157–160

Coca ceremonies, 15–19, 125–131, 134, 160–163, 203, 204–205

Coca leaves, 16–17, 120, 129, 185

Coincidence, 12–13, 28, 33–34, 38, 131, 156–157

Condor medicine, 165–166. *See also* Vilca trees

Consciousness

    author's revelation on, 62, 160–163, 190–191

    during ceremonies, 43–44, 64, 144–145, 193. *See also* Ayahuasca; Ayahuasca ceremonies

    importance of, 159–160, 173–175, 198–199, 202–207, 210–214

    during reimmersion, 202–203

Crohn's disease, 34–37, 72, 73, 95–96, 158

Cupping technique, 97–98

Curandero. *See* Shamans and shamanism

D

Dagura tribe, 167

Dan, 32, 57, 71, 86, 92–93, 104–105, 107, 153–154

Death

fear of, 115, 120–121, 208

medicinal herbs and, 2, 141–142, 165–166, 180

of patient, 111–115

tribal connections and, 167

Depression, 144–145, 158

Diabetes, 75, 83, 93–95

Dieta

Amazonian medicine approach through, 74–76, 78–79

for cancer, 99–102

for Crohn's disease, 95–96

for diabetes, 93–95

distractions and, 72–73, 75–79, 105–106, 152, 172–173

for Parkinson's disease, 96–99

for patients, 93–102

plant spirits and, 82–83

for production crew, 103–105, 106–107

as purification process, 86

reverence and, 108–110

strictness of, 91–92, 105–107

Distractions, 72–73, 75–79, 105–106, 152, 172–173

Dogs, 168–171, 182

Domestication, 168–173, 182–183

E

Edwin (shaman)

in closing ceremony, 158, 159

in coca ceremony, 125–131

at patient's death, 112–114

as shaman candidate for film, 62, 64–68

as vegetalista, 66–68, 83–87, 152–153

Ego

author's personal experience with, 8–14, 18–19, 38–42, 179–180, 185–191, 204–210

defined, 12–13

eye contact and, 18, 144–145, 148–150

letting go of, 3, 11–15, 42–44, 46–48, 51–52, 60–62, 152, 196–198

spiritual training protocol for countering, 210–214. *See also* Dieta

Eliade, Mircea, 136

Elrose, Frances, 108–110

Elton, 11, 17–18, 177–179, 182–183, 184, 197–198

Emotional Freedom Technique (EFT), 26–27, 29

Enawene Nawe tribe, 167

Epictetus, 135

"Everything is medicine" approach, 14–15, 134–136, 158, 197, 198–199, 213–214

Evolution, personal. *See* Spiritual training and evolution

Exorcism, 193

Externalities

distractions as, 72–73, 75–79, 105–106, 152, 172–173

illusion of separation as, 4, 7,
51–53, 146, 168, 173–176,
189, 204–205

Eye contact, 17–18, 87, 88, 144–145,
148–150, 174, 216

F

Fairies, 194, 197

Fear

consciousness and, 160–163

of death, 115, 120–121, 208

letting go of, 9–11, 13, 40, 51–52,
55, 190–191

opening up about, 188

Filming. *See Sacred Science, The* (film)

Fire ants, 2

Forgetfulness, 212

Freud, Sigmund, 12

G

Garlic and lemon tonic, 49–50, 186

Garry (patient)

death of, 111–115

family's reaction to death of,
118–119

outlook of, 99–101

patients' reaction to death of,
116–117

Gianni, Kevin, 28–30

Gibran, Khalil, 21

Grandfather San Pedro, 48, 137–141,
142, 145–146, 166, 181

Grandma Ayahuasca. *See* Ayahuasca;
Ayahuasca ceremonies

Graviola, 83

Great-Grandfather Vilca, 165–166

Gretchen (patient), 73, 116, 117, 138,
145, 157

Guayusa, 95–96

H

Habin (shaman)

clearing ceremony performed by,
119–120

in coca ceremony, 125–131

on death, 120

herbal knowledge of, 66, 83, 125

neurological disorder specialty of,
64, 98, 140–143

at patient's death, 112–113

as shaman film candidate, 62–64

work with Nicola, 140

Hanis, Roman. *See* Roman (shaman)

Healing, defined, 2

Herbs, medicinal. *See* Medicinal herbs

Hippocrates, 54, 91

Hogan, Linda, 137

Hot/cold techniques, 48, 51–52, 53–54

Huachuma, 48, 137–141, 142, 145–
146, 166, 181

I

Illusions

of separation, 4, 7, 51–53, 146, 168,
173–176, 189, 204–205

of success, 205–206

Ingerman, Sandra, 201

Interconnections, personal. *See* Tribal connections

Inti Raymi, 193

Irritable bowel syndrome (IBS), 73, 157

Isolation, as healing protocol, 72–73, 75, 76–79, 102. *See also* Dieta

Itininga, 84

J

Jessica (patient), 73, 95–96, 116, 158

Joel (patient), 75, 83, 93–95, 101

John (patient), 76, 101–102, 117, 145, 146–148, 153–155, 157–158

Juan (patient), 83, 144–145, 158

Jung, Carl, 31

Jungle medicine. *See* Amazon rain forest; Ayahuasca; Ayahuasca ceremonies; Coca ceremonies; Coca leaves; Dieta; Medicinal herbs; *Sacred Science, The* (film); San Pedro ceremonies

K

Kafka, Franz, 71

Keller, Helen, 55

L

Letting go
during ayahuasca ceremonies, 42–44, 46–48, 193, 196–198

of ego. *See* Ego

"everything is medicine" approach to, 135–136

of fear, 9–11, 13, 40, 51–52, 55, 190–191

of fear of death, 115, 120–121, 208

of illusions. *See* Illusions

technique for, 14–15

Lightning, 123, 128, 129, 130–134

Lupuna, 85–87

M

Maloka, 87, 124

Mapacho, 86, 125, 142, 194

Martinez, Dennis, 87–89

Medicinal herbs. *See also specific medicinal herbs*

animal spirits of, 146, 166

ayahuasca. *See* Ayahuasca; Ayahuasca ceremonies

coca. *See* Coca ceremonies; Coca leaves

collecting, 83–87, 88–89

local, importance of, 87–89

poultices, 83, 152–153

spirits and energetics of, 81–83

teacher and power plants, 141–142

Medicine questions, 198–199

Medicine walks, 83–87, 88–89

Melinda (patient), 83, 117, 152–153

Melville, Herman, 160

Mermaids, 128

Mescalito medicines, 48, 137–141, 142, 145–146, 166, 181

Metaphysical space, 209

Michelle (Polizzi), 32, 57–58, 60–61, 71, 91–92, 107, 169–170

Mileen, 8–10, 17–18, 177–179, 184, 187, 191–192

Mosquitoes, 1, 77

Mucura, 84

Muir, John, 14

Multi-generational tribes, 167–168

N

Nakedness, 51–53, 173–174

Nature immersion exercise, 14–15

Neuroendocrine cancer, 99–101, 111–115

Nicola (patient), 64, 75, 96–99, 140–143

Nin, Anaïs, 151

O

Oak trees, 88

Offerings, to spirit gods, 16, 17, 120, 184–185, 202

Ortner, Nick, 25–26, 28–30

Outcast consciousness, 161–162

P

Pachamama, 46, 86, 102, 131, 190, 193, 208–209, 215–216

Paititi Institute
  ascent through, 177–180
  descent to, 7–11, 12–13, 183–185
  description of, 7–8, 11, 13
  film of. See Sacred Science, The (film)
  permaculture farming at, 181–183

Palo santo, 40, 120, 194–195

Papailla, 95

Parkinson's disease, 75, 96–99, 140–143

Patients. See also specific names of patients
  addiction patient, 83, 144–145, 158
  applying to be, 55–58
  breakthroughs for, 151–160
  cancer patients, 76, 83, 84, 99–102, 111–115, 145–147, 152–155
  Crohn's disease patient, 73, 95–96, 116, 158
  death of, 111–115
  depressed patient, 83, 144–145, 158
  dieta for, 93–102. See also Dieta
  family's reaction to patient's death, 118–119
  IBS patient, 73, 116, 117, 138, 145, 157
  importance of stories in films, 4, 29–30
  Parkinson's disease patient, 75, 96–99, 140–143
  physical transformations of, 152–157
  reactions to patient's death, 116–117
  type 2 diabetes patient, 75, 83, 93–95, 101

Pendell, Dale, 177

Pendulum of experiences
  Amazonian medicine approach to, 76
  in ayahuasca ceremonies, 46–48, 197–198
  hot/cold therapy and, 51–52

Permaculture farming, 181–183

Personal evolution, 4, 40, 134, 159–160, 210–214, 215–216

Phenethylamine alkaloids, 138

Plantain chips, 92, 106–107

Plants, medicinal. *See* Medicinal herbs

Plant spirits, 81–83

Plotkin, Mark, 81

Poison, disease as, 135–136, 197

Polizzi, Michelle, 32, 57–58, 60–61, 71,
    91–92, 107, 169–170

Polizzi, Nick

    ayahuasca ceremony experiences,
        38–49, 188, 190, 192–198

    Catholic upbringing of, 21–23, 196

    chronic migraines of, 24–27

    coca ceremony experience of, 125–
        131, 160–163

    dread of ayahuasca ceremonies,
        18–19, 179–180, 185–191

    ego issues, 8–14, 179–180, 204–207

    letting go of fear, 9–11, 13, 40,
        51–52, 115, 120–121, 190–191,
        208

    life calling of, 4, 27–30, 134

    life-changing events of, 130–131

    lightning strike incident, 131–134

    on mortality, 115

    at patient's death, 111–115

    on raising children, 190–191,
        215–216

    rebirthing of, 60–62

    reimmersion in modern world,
        202–203

    return to Paititi Institute, 7–11

    role in patient's narrative, 154–155

    San Pedro ceremony experience,
        144–146

    sister of, 22–24

on spirituality, 215–216

Poultices, herb, 83, 152–153

Power plants, 141–142

Pretel, Oswald, 93–102

Primordial essence, 139

Prostate cancer, 76, 101–102, 153–155

Pumas, 146, 166. *See also* Andean
    cactus

Purification of spirt and body, 53–54

R

Radiation therapy, 153

Rage, 102, 160–163, 211

Rain forest. *See* Amazon rain forest

Rainy season, 151–152

Relámpago, 130. *See also* Lightning

Religion, 16, 21–24, 115, 196, 215–216

Respiratory illnesses, 88

Reverence, 108–110, 185

Rilke, Rainer Maria, 7

Roman (shaman)

    apprenticeship of, 37

    author's first meeting encounter
        with, 38

    as author's teacher, 38, 51–53, 87,
        162–163, 178–180, 186–187,
        190, 203–205

    in ayahuasca ceremonies, 39–42,
        47–49, 62–63, 192–195,
        197–198

    ayahuasca ceremony advice and
        warnings, 37, 39

    as candidate for *The Sacred Science*
        film, 33–34

    in closing ceremony, 158–160

in coca ceremony, 15–19, 125–131, 134

flora knowledge of, 66

healing journey of, 34–37, 95–96

healing protocol of, 62, 72–73, 74–78, 93–95, 97–102, 153–154, 213

on patient applications, 57

at patient's death, 112–115

on raising children, 215

retreat center of. *See* Paititi Institute

in San Pedro ceremonies, 138–141, 144–148

on toé use, 142–143

S

Sacred deposit slots, 184–185

Sacred Science, The (film)

arrival of patients, 73–74

clearing ceremony in, 119–120

closing ceremony in, 157–160

free viewing of, 156

healing protocol in, 73–78, 91–107. *See also* Dieta

importance of patient stories in, 4, 29–30

intentions for, 6, 129–130, 156

location for, 32–33, 71, 74

logistics for, 71–73, 93, 123–124

medical team for, 58, 72, 93

medicinal herbs and, 81–87. *See also* Medicinal herbs

patients in. *See* Patients; specific names of patients

production team for, 32, 71, 102–103

in rainy season, 151–152

reactions to, 18, 187–188

San Pedro ceremony in, 137–141, 144–148, 154

shamans in. *See* Edwin; Habin; Roman

synchronicity and, 12, 33–34

Sangre de grado, 95–96

San Pedro ceremonies, 137–141, 144–148, 154. *See also* Andean cactus

Santa Maria (plant), 67

Schultes, Richard, 141

Self-identification, 11–15

Self-preservation instincts. *See* Ego

Separation, illusion of, 4, 7, 51–53, 146, 168, 173–176, 189, 204–205

Sexual abstinence, 105–106

Shadow work, 27, 78–79, 162–163, 174–175

Shamans and shamanism. *See also* Edwin; Habin; Roman; Sinchi, Don

anthropologic evidence of, 5

blocks, removal of. See Blocks

ceremonies. *See* Ayahuasca; Ayahuasca ceremonies; Clearing ceremonies; Coca ceremonies; Coca leaves; San Pedro ceremonies

charlatans and, 68–70

consciousness and, 159–160

on death, 115, 120

defined, 4–5

"everything is medicine" approach, 14–15, 134–136, 158, 197, 198–199, 213–214

exploitation and, 88–89

film on. *See* Sacred Science, The (film)

healing tradition protocol. *See*
Dieta

lightning strikes and, 131

medicinal herbs and. *See* medicinal
herbs

oppression of, 6, 33, 88–89

primal truths of, 18, 45–46, 120–
121, 159–160

research for film project on, 31–32

rites of passage for, 37, 48, 85–87,
135–136

transfer of knowledge on, 5–6, 37,
83–87, 88–89

Shushupe, 92–93

Sinchi, Don, 35–37, 72–73

Smoke clearing ceremonies, 119–120

Snakes, 92–93, 166. *See also* Ayahuasca

Souls, 114

Spiritual training and evolution

distraction removal techniques,
78–79. *See also* Dieta

"everything is medicine" approach,
14–15, 134–136, 158, 197,
198–199, 213–214

eye gazing technique, 148–150. *See
also* Eye contact

hot/cold therapy techniques, 48,
51–52, 53–54

letting go techniques, 14–15,
173–175. *See also* Illusions;
Letting go

local medicinal herbs and, 89

medicine questions, 198–199

reverence for, 108–110, 185

shadow work techniques, 27,
78–79, 160–163, 174–175

training ground for, 210–214

Stagnation, 208

Steam bath, 53–54

Stella, 11, 18, 186, 192–193, 195–198

Stone deposit slots, 184–185

Substance abuse, 158

Success, illusion of, 205–206

Sweat lodges, 48, 53–54

Synchronicity, 12–13, 28, 31, 33–34,
38, 131, 156–157

T

Tahuari trees, 95

Tarahumara tribe, 210

Teacher plants, 141–142

Teas, 67, 83, 104

Technology, as distraction, 77, 78–79,
167, 172–173

Temazcal, 53–54

Toé, 98, 141–143

Tribal connections

defined, 166

domestication's effect on, 168–173,
182–183

illusion of separation and, 4, 7,
51–53, 146, 168, 173–176,
189, 204–205

multi-generational, 167–168

resistance to, 157, 201

shared experiences creating, 49–50

societies and, 166–167

Twain, Mark, 123

Twin sister, loss of, 63–64

Type 2 diabetes, 75, 83, 93–95

U

Ulcers, 66–67

Uña de gato, 83, 95–96

V

Vegetalista, 66–68, 83–87, 152–153

Vilca trees, 142, 165–166, 189

Vine of souls. *See* Ayahuasca; Aya-
    huasca ceremonies

Vulnerability, 18–19, 49, 152, 162–163,
    173–175, 208

W

Wetness, of rainy season, 151–152

Words, power of, 10–11, 42, 44–45,
    46–47, 159

Y

Yãkwa ritual, 167

ACKNOWLEDGMENTS

Everything I do creatively winds up a family affair, whether they like it or not. Without my brilliantly talented and loving tribe, this book would not have been possible.

Thank you, Mom, for bringing me into this world and showing me how to be fiercely compassionate but also discerning—you are always the first person I show rough drafts to because I trust your intellect and understanding of who I am. To my older sister, Liz, who edited this book—*three* times—I've been looking up to you since I was zero, so handing you the literary reins felt preordained. Thank you for the days of work you put into this. To my pop, thank you for being an unwavering support system to me always—I wrote this with the spirit of your intellect sitting on my shoulder, prodding me to include more descriptors and supporting data when things felt a little "thin." To my soul brother Mark DeRespinis, who pulled back the veil of this reality and invited me to take a peek 15 years ago—honored to be on this path with you. To my lifelong friends Nick Ortner and Kevin Gianni (order of appearance is not an indicator of preference)—thank you for holding me accountable to my purpose on this planet, and for keeping the bond strong. To my poolside conspirators Pedram Shojai and Jeff Hays—your candidness, humor, and creative genius never cease to inspire.

Thank you, Roman Hanis, for helping me see what *this* all truly is, and for holding space for my—at times—agonizingly slow spiritual growth. Not sure how we find ourselves in this cosmic dance, but I'm honored to be here.

Thank you to Reid Tracy and Patty Gift from Hay House for putting your faith in this book and for giving me the freedom to venture "off the reservation" when the subject matter called for it. Grateful for the opportunity.

Thank you to Sandra Kring—for taking me under your wing in the 11th hour, schooling me in the art of storytelling, and helping me navigate the home stretch. Thank you to Shannon Kring Buset—for all the work you do on behalf of indigenous communities across the Americas, and for being a true friend.

Thank you to Mileen Patel and Deb Larrabee—your tireless dedication to serving the Sacred Science community is such a gift. Without you two, none of this would be possible.

To Dan Bailey—we had no idea what we were getting ourselves into with the Sacred Science film, and you were willing to step off the ledge with me. Thank you for that. And an additional thank-you to Dan for being one of the funniest people on planet Earth. To Carl Bailey—thank you for believing in us.

To Brock Bertloff—thank you for all the time and love you put into each frame of the *Sacred Science* film and for living out the lessons we learned in the jungle.

My deepest gratitude goes to my beloved wife, Michelle Polizzi. My work is your work. We've shared a bigger vision for this world since our 20s, and little by little the evolution is starting to happen. Thank you for booting me out the door every time the medicine comes knocking. I'm humbled and inspired by the unbounded love you have for me and our two boys.

Lastly, thank you, dear reader, for understanding that you're more than the flesh, bone, and blood that has been turning these pages. Your quest for truth in this existence is contagious. Don't stop.

No matter what.

ABOUT THE AUTHOR

Nick Polizzi has spent his career directing and producing feature-length documentaries that explore the power of traditional medicine. His quest for ancient cures has taken him around the world into remote cultures that still practice these fast-disappearing methods. Nick's current role as founder of the online community the Sacred Science stems from a calling to honor, preserve, and protect the knowledge and rituals of the indigenous peoples of the world.

Website: www.theSacredScience.com

Hay House Titles of Related Interest

YOU CAN HEAL YOUR LIFE, the movie,
starring Louise Hay & Friends
(available as a 1-DVD program, an expanded 2-DVD set,
and an online streaming video)
Learn more at www.hayhouse.com/louise-movie

THE SHIFT, the movie,
starring Dr. Wayne W. Dyer
(available as a 1-DVD program, an expanded 2-DVD set,
and an online streaming video)
Learn more at www.hayhouse.com/the-shift-movie

■ ■ ■

BEYOND RAIN OF GOLD, by Victor Villaseñor

*CAVES OF POWER: Ancient Energy Techniques for Healing,
Rejuvenation and Manifestation,* by Sergio Magaña

KINDLING THE NATIVE SPIRIT: Sacred Practices for Everyday Life,
by Denise Linn

ONE SPIRIT MEDICINE: Ancient Ways to Ultimate Wellness,
by Alberto Villoldo, Ph.D.

SACRED POWERS: The Five Secrets to Awakening Transformation,
by davidji

All of the above are available at your local bookstore,
or may be ordered by contacting Hay House (see next page).

■ ■ ■

We hope you enjoyed this Hay House book. If you'd like to receive our online catalog featuring additional information on Hay House books and products, or if you'd like to find out more about the Hay Foundation, please contact:

Hay House, Inc., P.O. Box 5100, Carlsbad, CA 92018-5100
(760) 431-7695 or (800) 654-5126
(760) 431-6948 (fax) or (800) 650-5115 (fax)
www.hayhouse.com® • www.hayfoundation.org

———

Published in Australia by:
Hay House Australia Pty. Ltd., 18/36 Ralph St., Alexandria NSW 2015
Phone: 612-9669-4299 • *Fax:* 612-9669-4144 • www.hayhouse.com.au

Published in the United Kingdom by:
Hay House UK, Ltd., Astley House, 33 Notting Hill Gate, London W11 3JQ
Phone: 44-20-3675-2450 • *Fax:* 44-20-3675-2451 • www.hayhouse.co.uk

Published in India by: Hay House Publishers India,
Muskaan Complex, Plot No. 3, B-2, Vasant Kunj, New Delhi 110 070
Phone: 91-11-4176-1620 • *Fax:* 91-11-4176-1630 • www.hayhouse.co.in

———

**Access New Knowledge.
Anytime. Anywhere.**

Learn and evolve at your own pace
with the world's leading experts.

www.hayhouseU.com

Free e-newsletters from Hay House, the Ultimate Resource for Inspiration

Be the first to know about Hay House's free downloads, special offers, giveaways, contests, and more!

 Get exclusive excerpts from our latest releases and videos from *Hay House Present Moments*.

 Our *Digital Products Newsletter* is the perfect way to stay up-to-date on our latest discounted eBooks, featured mobile apps, and Live Online and On Demand events.

 Learn with real benefits! *HayHouseU.com* is your source for the most innovative online courses from the world's leading personal growth experts. Be the first to know about new online courses and to receive exclusive discounts.

 Enjoy uplifting personal stories, how-to articles, and healing advice, along with videos and empowering quotes, within *Heal Your Life*.

 Have an inspirational story to tell and a passion for writing? Sharpen your writing skills with insider tips from *Your Writing Life*.

Sign Up Now!

Get inspired, educate yourself, get a complimentary gift, and share the wisdom!

Visit www.hayhouse.com/newsletters to sign up today!

 HAY HOUSE

 HAYHOUSE RADIO
radio for your soul®

 HAYHOUSE online learning